Multi-Site Churches

Guidance for the Movement's Next Generation

Scott McConnell

B&H
PUBLISHING GROUP
Nashville, Tennessee

To every church leader who is seeking God's will
for their church related to multi-site.

Contents

Acknowledgments

First, thank you to Thom Rainer and Brad Waggoner for leading LifeWay Research to explore multi-site churches. As we discussed this possibility, Chuck Carter, Todd Atkins, and Brian Frye were instrumental in motivating LifeWay Research to move forward.

To the LifeWay Research team without whom this project could not have been accomplished: Lizette Beard, Courtney Eichelberger, Keith Pipes, and Carmen Comeaux for arranging and conducting interviews. Thanks to Sandra Wilson and Shirley Cross for helping me juggle my schedule to keep other research projects moving throughout the writing.

To those we interviewed at the participating multi-site churches (see page 238): this journey is one I never expected to seek. Ultimately it was your candid insights and moving testimony of God's work that motivated me to write this book. This became more than simply a new set of research findings. It became a story of God's movement that needed to be told and guidance for which many churches have asked.

To each contributor who believed in this book and shared your experience and wisdom: James MacDonald, Dave Ferguson, Geoff

Surratt, Rick Rusaw, Jimmie Davidson, Scott Chapman, Dino Rizzo, Jon Ferguson, and Warren Bird.

To Ed Stetzer for investing in me through this project and allowing me to devote so much of my time to this particular project.

To the outstanding team at B&H Publishing Group, especially Thomas Walters, who believed in this message and was determined to share this guidance with churches.

A special thanks to my wife, Debbie, and my children, Madison and Max. Thank you for sharing me with this project throughout the last year. As much as I enjoy my work, you mean so much more to me!

I pray that God will be magnified through the stories of these churches.

Foreword

Many of us have wanted to be in two places at once. At times, you just need to take care of business in multiple spots. Some churches are feeling that frustration and are meeting the challenge head-on. They see multiple fields of ministry and no longer feel the need to choose one over the other. So they are pursuing a multi-site model.

In June 2008 I posted three blog entries (www.edstetzer.com) on the multi-site movement, and it gained a lot of attention. Now, to be transparent, currently I preach at a multi-venue church every week. But I believe it is necessary to think through the consequences, intended and unintended, of any new approach to church. The multi-site church is a movement that I find to be fascinating because of its potential impact—and potential weaknesses. Currently I find myself in a torrent of opinions about multi-site because some of my friends are leading them and others of my friends are suspicious of them.

Many great leaders like Geoff Surratt and Aubrey Malphurs are writing about the subject, adding great information to the ongoing dialogue.

Even *World Magazine* presented an article highlighting the burgeoning movement surveying both the enthusiasm and concerns about the multi-site model. And there are definitely some strong opinions on both sides.

In this book you will find the information necessary to take a step back and survey the ministry landscape of multi-site churches. Scott McConnell's research and conclusions presented in the following pages will help you see the strengths of the multi-site movement. So where do we begin to look at such a new movement?

My Shop, Their Shop

First, we need to get a grip on exactly what *it* is. You might take a look at a coffee shop. Local coffee shops take years to establish a clientele and most people will never know they even exist—even if it is a great coffee shop. But if a national chain—say a place called Buckstops—opens a store on the other side of town, everyone knows about it immediately. Why? Because it has an established reputation, people know what they will get when they go in, and it has a familiar feel to the experience.

Many congregations are moving to a multi-site strategy for this reason: a new church may take years to get a footing, but an extension site of an established church will grow immediately. Instead of starting with twenty attendees, they may start with hundreds. (For example, when Andy Stanley and North Point started the Browns Bridge campus of North Point, thousands showed up the first day.)

Scott McConnell's book will help us gain a better understanding of why this can be an effective model for the church today. The research and conclusions drawn by Scott will help church leaders make the decision whether or not multi-site ministry is right for their church. It is not just a matter of franchising your church out to the masses. This book shows how your church can establish a detailed plan for moving toward this model of church life.

My Honest Concerns

Without question, all models of ministry have their challenges. The multi-site model is no different. In pursuing effective multi-site ministry, let me point out three potential challenges you must consider and how to overcome them.

First, pastoral responsibilities can get lost in the mix of a multi-site church. The scriptural assignments of praying over the sick (see James 5:14); watching over those placed in your care (see 1 Pet. 5:1–3); and discipline (see 1 Cor. 5) are duties assigned to a campus pastor, but we also know it often does not happen. The temptation to primarily focus on the worship service event can lead to a personal disconnection between the shepherd and sheep.

Second, in the bid to expand the size of a congregation, true Christian community can be compromised. One of the challenges of the multi-site model is that it can encourage a "come-and-get it" mentality over a come-and-give ethos and a go-and-tell mission. Our faith community should be one that desires to serve one another. If you are going to be multi-site, then you must give the people ample opportunities to serve one another all week long.

Third, and I think most important, is the potential limitations on reproducing leaders. Let's face it—it's easier to create another extension site than it is to create another Andy Stanley, Larry Osborne, or Greg Surratt. Fortunately for the church as a whole, men like these are actively raising up new leaders. But there is a temptation to simply have the campus pastor push the play button for your DVD sermons. It seems to me that our Great Commission strategy should include the reproduction of biblical communicators.

There are challenges to the multi-site model. Every new innovation has unintended side effects. That's one of the reasons that LifeWay Research looked at the multi-site approach. It is also one of the reasons for this book. There are churches failing at multi-site ministry because of these and other challenges. But there are others working through—overcoming these and other challenges—and we wanted to learn from them. This book is the result.

Throughout Scott's book, he will address my concerns, your concerns, and some we have not even thought of yet. His research led to interaction with many multi-site church leaders who are solving these problems and leading other churches to do the same.

My Hopeful Outlook

I am unashamedly anti-consumerism when it comes to the church. The bride of Christ ought to be the place where God's glory is made manifest to a world darkened by sin. When all we do is work for a larger number of attendees, we have failed in the mission of God. Scott's work will help us all in leading our churches away from being purveyors of religious "goods and services." Instead, it will point us toward reproduction as the goal—reproducing believers, ministries, groups, and churches. If you are going multi-site, stay focused on the mission and its multiplication.

Throughout this book, my colleague and the brains of LifeWay Research, Scott McConnell, will help you think through these and many other issues. He lays out his insights gained through a biblical perspective and rigorous research. Whether you are simply thinking about the issue, have committed your church to the model, or are in the middle of a multi-site church, this book will certainly provide solutions to many of the problems multi-site churches are facing or could face.

—Ed Stetzer

Introduction

My personal journey with multi-site began with my own pastor's vision. Poly Rouse planted the seed with our congregation several years ago that he felt God calling Hermitage Hills Baptist Church to be a multi-site church. I distinctly remember thinking how little I knew about this and how far off it seemed.

The timing of our pastor's revelation was interesting: we were about to move into a brand new sanctuary that would likely take several years to fill. By the time the pastor mentioned it again, probably a year later in an annual vision sermon, I was at least familiar with the concept through things LifeWay's consultants were learning in their interactions with some of these churches. Few in our congregation had probably given it much thought over the course of that year.

Less than a year later, God had prepared a second site for Hermitage Hills. Now as I write this, we are beginning tangible preparations for a third site. Serving on a ministry team that is helping the staff prepare for this third site (and future sites after that) has prompted many questions of my own. It has been easy to place myself in the shoes of those who want to learn from those who have already experienced the things we soon will need to decide and do.

This research project began to be discussed the first official month LifeWay Research existed. In October 2006 we sat down with Chuck Carter from First Baptist Windermere, Todd Atkins from McLean Bible Church, and Brian Frye, a doctoral student at Southern Baptist Theological Seminary.

Our discussion centered on what research we could do that would help multi-site churches or those considering becoming multi-site churches. Two needs emerged from our discussion: quantifying the activities currently underway among multi-site churches and providing practical assistance to those churches considering becoming multi-site.

> *The survey revealed that 16 percent of Protestant pastors indicate that their church is "seriously considering adding a worship service at one or more new locations or campuses in the next two years."*

We soon learned that Leadership Network was about to field their second major survey of multi-site churches, which would accomplish the first need. I attended the Coast to Coast Multi-Site Conference at North Coast Church in Vista, California, to be among the first to see this data in February 2007. Their data and many of the speakers affirmed the diversity of methods being used among multi-site churches.

LifeWay Research conducted a survey in April–May 2007 among 1,005 Protestant pastors who affirmed the second need. The survey revealed that 16 percent of Protestant pastors indicate that their church is "seriously considering adding a worship service at one or more new locations or campuses in the next two years."

Clearly one out of six churches would not become multi-site in those next two years. However, the multi-site movement had garnered enough attention that 16 percent of churches would be taking a good, hard look at it. In December 2008 we asked this question again among 1,004 Protestant pastors. Interest in multi-site remains strong as 15 percent are seriously considering adding a worship service at a new campus within the next two years. This book was birthed from this need—to provide practical advice to those considering or embarking on this journey.

But Leadership Network's research indicated it could be a challenge. Would there be enough common ground among the diverse multi-site stories to provide practical recommendations?

My experience with many research projects over the years in ministry, business, and consumer settings is that common needs, challenges, and solutions do emerge when a systematic interview process is utilized. So we conducted in-depth interviews with forty multi-site churches from across the country. We spoke with first-generation multi-site churches who blazed the trail and second-generation, early adopters who have done a lot of thinking about multi-site as they joined the movement.

We heard firsthand stories of their journey into multi-site. We specifically asked them to share the challenges they faced, so that the next generation of multi-site churches could be better prepared. Multi-site churches were very willing to participate and proved to be quite candid. For a complete list of interviewees and churches, see page 238.

Each of us likes to view our church as unique in much the same way we view ourselves as unique. While this is ultimately true, many of the attributes that together make our church unique are actually shared with many other churches. Each dimension of church life that we share with other churches provides us an opportunity to learn from others like us.

Forty first- and second-generation multi-site churches. Nine multi-site experts. One book. That's more than fifty opportunities to learn.

Some will find specific examples are harder to learn from because the church is "so different" in another area of their ministry. That's why we interviewed so many churches. There will be some "just like your church." However, there will also be principles from each situation that will inform the decisions you will face.

Some of the findings will be cut-and-dry: Here is the right way to do it and here is the wrong way to do it. However, other findings will be dependent on other decisions you make along the way.

This search for commonalities could sound like a quest to over-simplify the process of becoming multi-site. Don't worry. The multi-site experts and I will be shooting straight with you. In fact, complexity will be reflected in the many findings that really fall into the realm of counting the cost.

God's leadership or tangible barriers in your context may dictate a direction. Research insights will reveal whether your path will be a little more difficult or easier based on the direction you take. Thinking through these realities will allow your church to know ahead of time how best to prepare and what to expect.

This book combines firsthand advice from nine multi-site experts, stories from forty multi-site churches, and many insights along with practical guidance to help you consider your multi-site journey. Your answers to the many decisions and questions in this book may just be the beginning of the story of your multi-site journey.

May this guidance allow your church to avoid some of the challenges and be more effective along the way.

CHAPTER ONE

Why Multi-Site?

As we interviewed a variety of multi-site churches, we started by asking them to share their story. What was their motivation for becoming multi-site? What were the circumstances around them becoming multi-site?

How about you? Why do you want to be on the multi-site journey?

Take a minute to think about that. Write down your motivation. This begins your story.

When Does Multi-Site Make Sense?

Several common principles emerged from the stories and advice of various multi-site churches. Test your motivations with these principles and the scriptural principles with which they parallel.

When the Focus Is on the Great Commission

Bridgestone Baptist Church had fallen on hard times and was unable to make their loan payment. As they explored different options, they contacted Spring Baptist Church about the possibility of becoming a second campus of Spring Baptist. Although Spring's pastor, Mark Estep, had gotten to know Bridgestone's pastor over the previous couple years, this was a new idea.

The idea was worth considering, yet Estep was troubled about whether it was the prudent thing to do. The timing didn't seem right, because Spring had just voted to build a new youth building. Estep wrestled with turning around and taking on another church as a responsibility.

As they committed this to much prayer, it seemed wise to tap into a special member of his church, T. W. Hunt, author of several books including *When God Speaks*. Estep recounted their conversation that day:

> So I took him to lunch with a couple of my staff. I told him, "T. W., I need to tell you something that we are really looking at right now. We are trying to discern God's will and we need your prayers." So I began to tell him. I said, "I have been asking, if we do this, what does it mean for Spring Baptist Church? And if we don't do it, what does it mean for Spring Baptist Church? If we do this, what does it mean for Bridgestone Baptist? And if we don't do it, what does it mean for Bridgestone Baptist?"
>
> And he responded by saying, "Well, Mark, you are asking the wrong question. You should ask, 'If you do this or don't do this, what does it mean for the kingdom?'"
>
> And when he asked me that, immediately I began to have God quicken my heart and I knew that it was God's will that we move forward with it.

Spring Baptist Church followed this wise advice and put the kingdom of God first in their thinking. They stepped out on faith to become multi-site when a single-church focus may have led to a different decision.

Multi-site churches are evangelistic. They have experienced growth and are growth oriented. In other words, their bent is to make decisions based on a desire for the kingdom of God to grow. The decision to add their second site and sometimes other sites since then was driven from this desire to reach people with the good news of Jesus Christ.

It is one thing for churches and individual Christians to want new people to come to faith in Jesus Christ. It is quite another thing for an individual and even a church to take ownership of this responsibility.

Brad Waggoner, in his book *The Shape of Faith to Come*, shares the results of a LifeWay Research survey of twenty-five hundred adults who attend a Protestant church at least once a month. He shares that among them only 46 percent agree strongly that they have a personal responsibility to share their religious beliefs about Jesus Christ with non-Christians.

Despite such reluctance to take this responsibility, ownership of this responsibility is clear in Scripture. Jesus told His disciples to go into all the world and preach the gospel (see Mark 16:15). It would be illogical to assume that Christ intended this command only for that first generation of followers. In the same way it would be illogical for any believer to assume that this responsibility is reserved for someone else.

We would expect Jesus' final prayer to be either a summary of His petition to God or the most important petition He could submit to God the Father. Jesus' final prayer prior to being arrested, recorded in John 17, indicates that Jesus desired that all believers be unified for one purpose, telling the world that God loves them enough to send Jesus to earth for their salvation.

This prayer confirms the necessity of involvement in a local church. Joining with other believers is not an option; it is the heart cry of our Savior. The focus of the church should be nothing less than sharing the message in both words and actions that God loves the world so much that He sent Jesus Christ to die for us.

The danger in examining any new method or program or style is that the new perspective could shift a church from its God-given evangelistic focus. A first-generation multi-site pastor, Chuck Carter, has seen many different churches consider becoming multi-site. He cautions,

"There has got to be something driving the thing. Among the churches I know where it is successful, it is because the Great Commission is driving it."

Your motivation impacts how you measure success. And there is no guarantee of success when a site is added.

Mike Brisson, associate pastor at Cornerstone Community Church, defined success as he shared his heart for how his Temecula campus needs to improve: "I don't want transfer growth from another church. I am not going to do it unless I can have kingdom growth, so I want people who don't go to any church; I want *them* to come to Temecula."

Every church that is focused on the Great Commission is not called to be a multi-site church, but every multi-site church should be driven by an evangelistic passion.

When You Have a Culture of Multiplication

Jesus shared the principle in the parable of the sower (see Matt. 13:1–9, 18–23) in which the one who planted reaped thirty, sixty, or one hundred times what had been sown. Today Sunday school leaders advocate that each teacher mentor another teacher so eventually they can have two classes. Likewise, in preparation for student ministry, future youth ministers are taught to invest most of their time in other leaders rather than trying to do the entire ministry with students themselves.

Most leaders agree with the principle. Few members enjoy it. Fewer churches do it. And even fewer churches have engrained multiplication into their culture, resisting the dividing rather than celebrating the addition.

Among the forty multi-site churches we studied, it was quite common to find multiplying engrained in their culture. For some, it truly didn't become a frequent thing until they became multi-site. Adding one or more sites creates a necessity for multiplication where previously it was simply "nice to have."

The purest form of a culture of multiplication that we saw is probably Christ the King Community Church. They began as an overflow service of a church with the same name thirty miles to their north in Bellingham, Washington. Despite rapid growth from the outset, their pastor, Dave Browning, told the people that "we are not going to ask everyone to keep coming to us. We are going to ask us to go to them."

This established in Christ the King a different kind of culture. "That began the journey that we are still on, which is launching other small groups, and cafés, and worship centers here, there, and everywhere." Browning summarizes their organic process: "We're asking everybody at every level to be multiplying.

"There is an emphasis given throughout our entire network on multiplying and launching new leaders, new services, and new sites. So that's what gets rewarded in our culture."

Executive Director of Business and Finance Dave Lonsberry describes the calling of Christ Fellowship Church: "One of the things that we really feel that we are called to do as a church is to help change our communities by sharing the gospel and seeing lives transformed so that those people can also then share the gospel with others—the multiplication effect."

When You Are Willing to Remove Logistical Barriers to Reach More People

Many of the forty churches had hit growth barriers, and they found multi-site as a way to continue the growth.

Cornerstone had already begun to use other strategies to address the limitations of their facility and parking. In the midst of the lengthy process of almost tripling their seating capacity with a new sanctuary, they began experimenting with a second venue, a different setting for worship that they called "Small Church." As its name indicates, it was a smaller setting (one hundred and twenty chairs). It was also a less formal worship service that offered coffee and refreshments in the back, and allowed people to stand up whenever they wanted to rather than on cue from the worship leader. Eventually they offered this venue during each of their four Sunday morning service times with live worship and a live video feed for the sermon. At that time, they also had two services on Saturday.

To continue to make room and create opportunities for growth, Cornerstone added being multi-site to their multiple services on multiple days with multiple venues. Each addition was with the goal of reaching more people. The new site, ten miles to their south, is in an area that they estimated had ninety thousand people who were not attending church. They opened this second site in a movie theater.

Besides space, the other barrier that several churches faced or anticipated facing was the financial barrier of building bigger buildings to accommodate growth.

Community Presbyterian Church weighed three options over time on how to deal with their growth. They could move the whole church from their downtown Danville, California location, they could build a fifteen-hundred-seat sanctuary, or they could add video venues and an "extension" or second site. The last cost they had calculated for the new sanctuary was well over $40 million. The finances of other growth options were prohibitive, leading them to become multi-site.

Similarly Crossroads Community Church had grown to the point where they had four weekend services: two on Saturday night and two on Sunday morning. Lead pastor Keith Boyer recalled that they, too, were asking, "Where do we go next? Do we add another service? Is it time to build another facility?"

As Crossroads began to look at the cost of building, they found they needed a $7 or $8 million facility. "For us, at that time, [this amount] was a pretty significant step of faith. We really had to look at it through the lines of what's faith? And what's presumption? And what's going to honor the people? And what's going to stretch them beyond what's appropriate? At that point, we said maybe we need to begin to think outside the box."

God had already supplied Crossroads with a great resource to do just that. Two of their key staff members had served with Greg Surratt, who is now senior pastor at Seacoast Church, a leading first-generation multi-site church, and coauthor of *The Multi-Site Church Revolution*. This relationship gave them a front-row seat to observe the things happening at Seacoast in the days that the approach was emerging.

As they began to think about the potential financial barrier of building a new facility, growing through adding sites began to make financial sense. Initially they thought they could launch a campus for $100,000 (it is more than $120,000 today). "Do the quick math on it. If it costs us $7 or $8 million to build a building, we can launch seventy-five campuses for that same amount and reach a whole lot more people closer to [their] home."

Each of these churches displayed a passion to reach people with the gospel that was greater than the barriers or traditional boundaries they faced. As they trusted God, they searched—much like a child trying different paths in a corn maze. When each direction seemed closed, God opened a new way. For these churches it included becoming multi-site.

When You Are Willing to Seize the Opportunity

Cedar Park became multi-site out of necessity. They did not want a nearby church in their denomination to close its doors, so they took on this site out of principle. This turned out to be just the first opportunity to add a location to their church. They now have seven "branches."

Cedar Park applies this willingness to act on opportunities to more than just adding additional sites or branches to their church. Their senior associate pastor, Craig Gorc, sums it up this way: "Our compelling vision and strategy is that we are going to partner with people who demonstrate a calling to ministry as much as we can."

When a retired man who attended Cedar Park was seeking a way to serve, they found he had years of experience starting Goodwill stores. About four months after the initial conversation, the church put money down on a 150,000 square foot warehouse that became Hidden Treasures Thrift Store, a thriving ministry that serves a great need in their community and allows Cedar Park to partner with other churches.

RiverTree Christian Church acted on the opportunity that no one else wanted. Associate pastor Don Ruppenthal explained their choice of their first new site: "Actually, the reason we did it is because we felt, 'If we don't, who will?' In fact, a lot of churches were abandoning the area and going out to the suburbs." RiverTree had members attending from that direction and saw that this downtown area needed a church. They launched a site "in a city where most of the churches are either not growing or they are shutting down."

Celebration Church is driven by opportunities. "We're willing to try anything," Celebration's lead pastor Stovall Weems said. "Our church has a very high change culture. It will be no big deal if we try something—a new service or a new venue—and then say, 'Well, OK, that didn't work like we thought. OK, we're doing *this* now.'"

Weems described Celebration's decision to go multi-site as anything but agonizing. "It was more like, OK, here's an opportunity. Let's go for it. Let's check it out and let's see where God takes it. And we can put some definition around it as it goes."

In contrast the culture at Evergreen Presbyterian was much more deliberate. Pastor Nathan Lewis describes that they anticipated that multi-site might be a future answer to growth hurdles. A year after groundbreaking on their first building in Beaverton, Oregon, they knew that overcoming that original debt would take time. Yet, they would want to continue to grow once this new building was filled.

"We were in a planning phase for about two years," Lewis described. "We were being very careful Presbyterians, so all of our session and deaconate were investigating and researching and praying."

Despite this long lead time of reading and praying, the decision to become multi-site came quickly when an opportunity arose.

Several members of Evergreen had moved about thirty minutes from the church, continuing to commute that distance each week for church. As their children started playing water polo in a club in their new community, the family opened their home on Friday nights for the boys to socialize.

God began to work among these teenage boys. Two asked if they could have a Bible study when they got together on Friday nights. The family agreed and soon those two boys professed faith in Christ and were asking to go to Evergreen to participate in the youth group. The boys' families were interested enough to join them.

When these original members petitioned the session to do something for these families in the Newberg area, the session responded. Lewis began preaching at Beaverton at 9:00 a.m. and Newberg at 11:00 a.m. each Sunday. Within the first year, he had baptized twenty-eight people connected to those teenagers on the water polo team.

Stovall Weems described the right situation as a church that is serious about reaching people, serious about expanding the kingdom of God, serious about building team leadership in your church, and your church is growing. In this situation, "multi-site is a huge tool to be able to reach more people."

When Does Multi-Site Not Make Sense?

Even though Weems considers himself a "huge believer in the multi-site concept," he didn't say it was for everyone. Even in his excitement to proclaim its value, he rattled off four things that must be present for multi-site to make sense.

When a church has evangelistic fervor, is multiplying leaders, is seizing ministry opportunities, and is experiencing growth, multi-site can open doors for these blessings to continue at an even faster rate.

The converse is also true.

When a church is not showing vital signs of growth, a passion for sharing the gospel and equipping people to step into new areas of ministry and does not have a natural tendency to seek kingdom growth, then multi-site will only magnify these weaknesses.

When You Are Trying to Create Growth Rather than Leveraging Existing Growth

Shortly after Impact Community Church had bought a building for their original campus, they rented space in a nearby hotel to set up a site as a video venue. As their lease expired a year later, they mercifully pulled the plug on this second location.

Was this church inept? Hardly. In its first five years of existence, it went from zero to five hundred in attendance.

Was this church incapable of reproducing? Nothing could be further from the truth. Before the church turned three-years-old, they planted a church that now has three hundred in attendance.

Were the church's motives wrong? Not in and of themselves. There is nothing wrong with wanting your church to grow. All of us have experienced a desire for our church to grow during a season or sometimes years of not seeing such growth. But having good motives does not guarantee you are moving in the right direction.

The pastor describes a situation in which Impact had only known rapid growth. After another surge that followed moving into their new building, they leveled off. Pastor Barry Smith recalls, "We jumped to like four hundred fifty to five hundred and then plateaued, and plateaued, and plateaued." As the frustration mounted, they tried harder. "We were racking our brains. . . . We were trying to do everything we could to grow. And I think that is one of the first things that we did wrong, because we did a video venue in order to grow . . . without momentum and without a real need to expand."

Impact had good intentions, but nothing in their story indicates that they were seeing God move in this direction. Without such clear indications that this was the path God was setting forth for their church, they were destined to struggle.

Another young campus pastor summarized, "If you are considering going multi-site, make sure you are making that move because you really feel that God is leading you there, not as just a pragmatic way to grow your church or your church influence."

As with any of the stories shared in this book, these struggles may be something God wanted Impact to experience to prepare them for future endeavors. God definitely used the second site to add a handful of new people to the kingdom and to their church.

Adding a site is not a surefire method for church growth in the same way adding any other program or technique does not guarantee church growth.

As Acts 2:47 says, "And *the Lord* added to their number daily" (emphasis added, NIV). Choose the wrench that fits the bolt God is turning near you. You simply need to determine if multi-site is the tool that fits.

When Your Church Is Not Healthy

Adding a site does not simply add an address to your church. It adds complexity. In turn, that complexity puts stress on your people and your processes. Pretty quickly a church's weaknesses are revealed.

Many of the struggles we share in this book are tied to weaknesses that preexisted going multi-site. For example:

- Cedar Park realized a couple years into multi-site that some of their challenges were tied to the need for more clear communication of their vision for the future and how they were pursuing this.
- Evergreen Presbyterian multiplied their organizational messiness when they added a site.
- Crossroads Community Church realized they had not trained people sufficiently to mobilize them into effective service.

Each of these churches has addressed these weaknesses, but not until after they became multi-site and after they had felt the pain.

Investing in the health of your church should be an ongoing process. Assessing the health of your church before launching a new site allows you to address problems once rather than twice.

When You Are Using Space Constraints Alone to Justify Adding a Site

Many of the churches who have gone multi-site first considered it because of space constraints. Christ the King saw they were approaching the "lid." Cornerstone was starting to plateau "due to limitations of our facility and our parking." First Baptist Windermere was "totally landlocked at the downtown campus, so to continue to grow we were going to have to do something."

While the limitations of current facilities may have been a need and may have led these churches to seek a solution, space constraints do not mean multi-site is the answer for your church. It is one option.

Planting churches, building larger buildings, adding services, adding venues at your current site, and relocating a campus are all still viable solutions today. Multi-site does not replace these other solutions. It adds one more possibility for consideration.

In fact, many of the churches in this study utilized more than one of these solutions. First Baptist Windermere has both added sites and relocated a campus. Several of the churches, including Community Presbyterian and Harvest Bible Chapel, have planted churches in addition to adding sites. Replacing or updating buildings has occurred at both the original and new sites among these churches.

Being landlocked, restrained by incompatible zoning laws, limited by available parking, or stunted by the size of existing buildings on your campus all require action. These symptoms have more than one remedy. The key is to determine God's plan for your church and His solution to such growing pains.

Why Multi-Site?

The multi-site strategy does not replace any other method of participating in kingdom growth. It does not replace church planting, personal evangelism, visitation programs, investing and inviting, servant evangelism, or evangelistic training.

By definition, multi-site involves starting a site somewhere other than your current campus. This quickly draws some comparisons to church planting. While many of the goals, experiences, and characteristics look similar, new sites and church plants are traveling different routes that require different vision, resourcing, and style of leadership.

Pastor David Parker at Desert Vineyard encourages leaders faced with this choice to be intentional about exactly what they are doing off-site. "Is this part of the bigger whole or is this something that is going to stand and exist on its own? Having real clarity from the beginning about what you are creating off-site is essential."

Desert Vineyard intentionally launched a site rather than planting a church. However, Parker indicates, "We have an open hand today. If this is something that needs to evolve and grow and become independent, then we are fine with that. But we are also thrilled with the kind of growth and the health that it has because it is tied to something bigger and with a deeper root system."

God sent the prophet Samuel to Jesse's house. After Jesse's family had consecrated themselves, Samuel sized up the options. Who could be better equipped to know a sure thing when he saw one than Samuel? Many reading this book practically live at church. Samuel actually did live at the temple since he was a boy. Yet Samuel's first choice, Eliab, was rejected.

By God's grace, I have been a follower of Jesus Christ longer than I have had my teeth. It is pretty humbling to see Samuel, who also answered God at an early age, land completely on the wrong page.

"The Lord does not look at the things man looks at. Man looks at the outward appearance, but the Lord looks at the heart." (1 Sam. 16:7 NIV)

As you approach a decision on multi-site, "guard your heart" (Prov. 4:23 NIV). Joe Stowell, the executive pastor at Harvest Bible Chapel, points out that multi-site has become "a cool thing to do." As a result, many churches are thinking about it. "If God is leading you to do it, then go for it. But I wouldn't do it just to do it. It's a lot of work, and I do think it's hard on the staff. Sometimes I wonder, are there people doing this that maybe don't need to do it, and who could have better focused their resources and efforts into deeper, better ministry where they are?

"I would tell people they really have to think and pray about 'why do they need to do this?'" Stowell advises, "Pray about it. Have the Lord lead you into it, but determine that first. Don't do it just to do it. It's not that fun."

Harvest Bible Chapel's carefulness almost borders on reluctance to use the multi-site tool. In contrast, The Chapel is proactive in planning to use the tool of multi-site while still waiting for God to provide each opportunity.

Scott Chapman, copastor of The Chapel, reminds us, "It is not an end to itself. Multi-site is a tool. It is a means to an end. We have been treating it like the end. It is not. It is a means. What can you do with the tool of multi-site? Nobody is asking that."

"Start with a clear understanding of the vision and purpose that God has given your church," advises Tim Davis, guest relations and multi-site director at Woodcrest Chapel. "If you can be clear that God has called you to a specific purpose in your community, a specific vision, and multi-site makes sense to accomplish that purpose as a tool, then you need to follow that vision and purpose and do it with all your heart and with all your church."

In addition to the guidance that I have drawn from the multi-site churches we interviewed, this book includes advice from nine multi-site experts. Their contributions provide an opportunity for them to tell a little bit more of their story and to expound on their advice.

The first contribution is from James MacDonald, senior pastor of Harvest Bible Chapel. As Harvest experienced God's movement in and through their church, they also received a clear nudge from God to become multi-site.

James MacDonald

senior pastor, Harvest Bible Chapel

It may come as some surprise, but Harvest Bible Chapel didn't have any big plans or strategy or even desire to go multi-site. God was blessing our church with growth, and we were completely over-loaded. We were meeting in a big old warehouse and were running six shuttle buses for four services.

Our response to our growth problem was to start planting churches. We had a vision to plant ten churches in ten years starting in 2000.

And so we started sending people out to plant churches. The first year we sent out two groups of three hundred people, and then we continued to send people out for each new church plant. The Lord has really exceeded all of our expectations, and here in 2008 we hope to have launched our thirtieth church.

We would send three hundred of our best leaders out. These wonderful people would go, and then new people would come in kind of on the first floor. Then we helped these new people grow as leaders, and we would send them out. Then even more would come in. Church planting is a wonderful, biblical thing to do that Harvest Bible Chapel is very committed to do. Yet as wonderful and as fruitful as it was to

---

see these people going out and establishing new churches, we found out that church planting did not solve our growth problems.

So, we sought to relocate our church to a larger location. Here in the northwest suburbs of Chicago the population is very dense. As we looked, we found that there were really no properties or locations available to us. Ultimately we ended our search. This was a dark time for our church as we honestly did not know what we were going to do.

Then out of nowhere the Lord provided for us a campus that was outside of our search area. Through the generosity of the Green family that owns the Hobby Lobby stores, we were given an eighty-acre campus with a 280,000 square foot building and a nine hundred-car parking garage. It was built in the mid 1990s for about $53 million, and they gave it to us for a dollar.

At first, we thought, "Wow! We'll just move our whole church out there." But the problem was it was too far away. We couldn't move our whole church a half an hour away. As the reality of this development sunk in, we realized we were forced to become a two-campus church.

Similar to our church plants, more than seven hundred people left the original campus in Rolling Meadows and went to launch the new campus in Elgin. Since then, their spaces have been filled at the original campus while the new campus has grown to more than thirty-five hundred people in attendance.

This all seems overwhelming looking back, but in the midst of all this a little church down in Niles, about a half an hour in the other direction, came to us. They only had about thirty-five people attending in a three hundred fifty-seat worship center. They hadn't had water in the baptistery in three years, nobody was getting saved, and really nothing was happening. And they said, "Can you help us?"

They agreed to disband their former church government. They voted to never vote again, and they accepted our elder form of government. We set them up as a video site, and we called it Harvest Bible Chapel Niles. Within about three years, this campus became packed out in four services with about eleven hundred people attending there every week.

Since that time one of the churches we planted ran into financial difficulty, and their elders agreed to come back into partnership with us. The church had dropped from eight hundred to five hundred in attendance and was facing bankruptcy. By providing leadership and Harvest's video teaching, they have rebounded to more than one thousand in attendance and have gotten into a new facility.

In addition, we had a number of people who had moved to Phoenix for retirement or semiretirement who couldn't find a similar church. This base of leadership was ready to plant a church and Harvest was willing to help. Initially the right pastor could not be found, so they utilized video teaching just like the other video services Harvest has. Now that the church has grown to more than two hundred fifty and has a pastor in place, it has become an autonomous church.

When we started to go into multi-site, our attendance was between five thousand and six thousand. And while we have continued to plant churches we now have almost eleven thousand in weekly attendance.

With such a tremendous story of God's provision, you may expect us to be outspoken proponents of multi-site. The truth is that we are reluctant participants in multi-site.

In my ministry, it is the getting there that has been the great thing, not the arriving. In the same way multi-site is a vehicle; it is not the destination. So, be careful not to covet multi-site. It is extremely complex. It is very draining. It is a ton of work.

Personally it has been a struggle to adjust to the diminishment of my role in shepherding a flock. I love the people that I am preaching to and frankly there is just something unsatisfying and not authentic about rushing away from the people that you just poured your heart out to so you can make it to another service at another site. It is also a challenge to feel like a pastor in a church that you never see and that only sees you on video.

Multi-site as a focus has a lot of merit and we have done it, but it is also important that it does not diminish the hard work of reproducing ourselves in the lives of others. Some people are uniquely gifted to preach, but I really believe that the principles of communicating God's Word are transferable to other gifted people. We have to be careful that when we are perpetuating satellites that we are not really saying, "It is all reproducible except me." That would be an abdication of our responsibility to do the harder work of raising up others.

Theologically I have no hesitation with multi-site. In fact, when I am up preaching, I will often say, "I'm glad that you are here today wherever you are worshipping. It doesn't matter where I am. All that matters is where you are and where God is, and He is right with you now as we open God's Word together." The manifest presence of God in the corporate gathering of His people is significant, not the physical location of the mouthpiece, so to speak.

There is definitely a multilocation dynamic to the church in Acts. And I don't see anything in Scripture that forbids it. And technology allows it and abundant fruitfulness tends to force it and church planting doesn't protect us from it. We arrived at it reluctantly because we can't discount it from Scripture.

As churches consider becoming multi-site, they must first be drawn into multi-site through an abundant fruitfulness at your single location. There should be evidence that there is demand for your ministry that exceeds the capacity of your current geographical location or facilities. If there isn't enough demand for your ministry to fill one building, who are you kidding? There won't be more demand on the other side of town either.

Second, if you are experiencing some kind of abundance by God's grace, then you must consider the best way to steward that abundance. For Harvest, that stewardship meant doing several other things before we utilized multi-site. We had reached the limitation of a facility that was really full four times each Sunday, and we were planting churches and it still did not solve the growth of our church. Only then, when an opportunity came to continue to grow the fruitfulness that we were experiencing, did we become multi-site.

Without the experience of seeing the abundance and stewarding the abundance at your single site, just going into adding sites because everyone else is doing it could be a really bad decision.

CHAPTER
TWO

The Pieces That Need to Come Together

O ne of the practical steps on the multi-site journey that this book is designed to help you with is counting the cost. Jesus asked, "For which of you, wanting to build a tower, doesn't first sit down and calculate the cost to see if he has enough to complete it?" (Luke 14:28). While affirming that this is a prudent way of making a business decision, Jesus used it to illustrate how everyone should count the cost of being His disciple.

Using the same prudence Jesus commended for a building project, we should count the cost of embarking on the multi-site journey. Due diligence is not just for lawyers: it is the responsible thing to do.

As an undergraduate in the Wharton School of the University of Pennsylvania, I took a course in Entrepreneurial Management. The most memorable part of the class was an entertaining professor. Professor David took great joy in asking a question, then looking intently at one student while calling on the name of a different student to answer it. This often left both students stuttering and befuddled.

I also remember Professor David gave us more than one team assignment to invent a new product or service. After hours of considering different possibilities, we would have to apply rigorous evaluation methods to our half-baked ideas. It took more than a little ingenuity to make your idea look possible in light of such practical thinking.

I didn't go into the class with a great business idea, and I didn't walk out of the class with one either.

What I did take with me was a huge dose of reality. I learned that there is a whole lot more to launching a business than a good idea. And you had better have a well-tested plan if you expect to get others to believe you have what it takes to launch a new business—especially the venture capitalists or banks that would finance it.

Launching a new site for a church has many similarities to launching a new business. Each requires lots of long hours, an entrepreneurial spirit, an aversion to the status quo, and a willingness to try new things, take risks, and sacrifice.

Just as the specifics of each business are different, a multi-site "venture" will differ considerably from business ventures.

Yet some of those same questions that prove to be good tests to the viability of a business plan, also prove to be good tests of the readiness to add a new church campus.

- What are your objectives?
- Who is your target market?
- What are the trends and competition like?
- What does your operating plan look like?
- Who is on your management team?
- What are your financials?
- What will you offer?
- What are the critical risks and potential solutions?

In one way or another, we will address each of these questions in this book. There is not a single cookie-cutter approach to making the move to multi-site—in the same way that businesses do not have a single way to add franchises.

However, there are a basic set of things that need to be in place to go multi-site. In the same way, businesses as diverse as Dunkin Donuts and Jiffy Lube have common milestones that had to be achieved to begin to franchise their concepts.

Among the common principles used to go multi-site are six that must be in place before you even build a detailed plan. In terms of milestones, this is Step 0.

We will apply these six tests of validity or readiness to go multi-site. These are questions for you to answer, but they are not about you. They are about what you are observing.

Do you see God's activity in these six areas?

1. Unanimity among leaders
2. Leader
3. Core group
4. Location
5. Systems and structures in place
6. Finances

Professor David was an entrepreneur himself. He knew that which he taught, not in a sense of book knowledge but experiential knowledge. With each potential venture, he and other entrepreneurs learn much from the questions that banks and venture capitalists ask about their business proposal.

The entrepreneur enters the meeting with the financier strongly hoping for their much-needed "yes" to provide financing. Often the "nos" bring something much more valuable: an opportunity to improve the model or the proposal. The financier's searching questions may lead to an adjustment of expectations, time line, or approach. The denial may even allow the entrepreneur to avoid a major catastrophe.

The savvy venture capitalist is not giving the entrepreneur a hard time just for kicks. They have learned how to ask revealing questions and to evaluate business proposals the hard way—they lost money on the mistakes of previous businesses in which they invested.

So who are the savvy venture capitalists in the multi-site world? We turn to the experiences of first- and second-generation multi-site churches. They are the ones who have gained their expertise by that same painful path to experiential knowledge. Only such knowledge yields practical advice.

The common elements among their experiences yielded the six items that make up Step 0. So step into their office and ask yourself where your church is in these six areas.

Evidence of God at work in these specific ways is confirmation that the time to move forward and join Him is emerging. God's lack of activity will indicate that you need to continue to wait or look for His activity in a direction other than multi-site.

The churches studied saw God at work in these areas and that triggered them to move beyond just talking about multi-site to tangibly preparing to go multi-site.

Are you seeing God's activity in these six areas?

Unanimity among Leaders

"The senior pastor and the staff have to be in favor of it," Mike Brisson at Cornerstone Community Church summarized. "They have to be on board with it, they have to understand how it works, and they have to understand how to address people's fears because people are fearful; people don't like change."

Community Presbyterian had read about conflicts other churches had faced between teams at the sites and the original campus. They were able to avoid those issues.

"If you don't have unanimity," Mike Miller, director of ministry support, warned, "and I mean UNANIMITY, with all the leadership, don't move." This can't be forced or mandated. There must be natural, genuine buy-in.

Pastor David Parker described the progression of the decision at Desert Vineyard. "We began talking about this first with our staff and our board. Then as discussion widened we brought it to those involved in lower tier leadership. So the discussion of going to this [multi-site] approach was held over a period of time: beginning with the staff and then to layleaders and then to the church as a whole."

If the staff of Desert Vineyard had been divided on whether multi-site was right, the board would never have agreed. If there was not acceptance among the layleadership, the church as a whole would not have been on board.

Decisions of this magnitude either survive or fail in the informal discussions rather than the formal presentations. When people have honest "one off" conversations about such a proposal, they will reveal if they are really on board. At each level people watch to see if their leaders are genuinely supportive of the idea.

If the conviction that God is leading your church to be multi-site is not shared by your top level of leadership, you are not ready to begin to communicate this direction to the next group in the communication process.

A Multi-Site Compromise

One church that we interviewed agreed to participate if their name was not included. The church became a multi-site church out of compromise. The church was in the heart of a city and needed more space. The staff wanted to buy land, and indeed an opportunity to buy 103 acres north of the original site emerged. However, the elders didn't feel that this was the right thing for several reasons, not the least of which was the central location of the church in the heart of the city that they did not want to give up. So they compromised and started another campus with the idea that they would eventually purchase land for the second campus.

The second site experienced good growth, yet the elders began to realize that it was beginning to function as a separate church. The church did not launch this site with a unified multi-site vision, so many of the decisions along the way resemble decisions typical of a church plant. For example, they hired a senior pastor for the second site with staffing that reported to him, and this staff had no connection to the original site's staff.

It is not surprising that they soon became disconnected. It has been a painful process for the church to pull the site back under the original church's authority, and questions still remain as to whether it will be able to stay there long term. The primary reason that this is still a question is because there still is no unity among the leaders of the church about a multi-site vision for this church. Without this common direction, further conflict is inevitable.

The importance of your church's leaders being in complete agreement can best be illustrated by sharing a crisis that one multi-site church experienced. We won't share their identity to avoid pinpointing a wrong that has been forgiven.

Divided Views of Multi-Site

This church had added a site through what is often called a "rescue" or "resurrection" model. A church of fewer than ten people deeded their property to and came under the leadership of this multi-site church.

Initially the multi-site church chose to utilize a rotation of preachers to fill the pulpit, some of whom were not ordained. A couple of key lay-leaders from the multi-site church took a real interest in this new site but also did not agree with this arrangement for preaching at the new site.

The two leaders went down to the state capitol, paid $50, and signed over the property title to the small church building to their own families. Then one of the two men who longed to be a minister himself went and told the tiny congregation that he was their new pastor. He shared that there was a new name for the church, a new direction, and that they were ready to go.

The handful of original members at this tiny church felt betrayed. The senior pastor of the large church got a phone call from one of the tiny church's members saying he had twenty-four hours to turn those two men around and reverse the title change or the members' attorney would be serving him papers. In the words of that senior pastor, "That nearly blew everything up."

The senior pastor and the rest of the principle leadership of the multi-site church sat down with the two men. It was not an easy meeting. The men were very cold about what had happened and didn't want to discuss it. But in the end, the man who had named himself the pastor went back to the state capitol, paid another $50, and reversed the title change.

The two leaders who had taken a different course than the rest of their church's leadership chose to leave the church. One couple from the new small site was also so disturbed by the episode that they left as well. This very difficult time for this particular multi-site church could have been much worse. The remaining members of the small new site trusted the church's leadership that they were committed to that site and were sticking with them.

This serious crisis occurred as leaders with different views on their church's multi-site approach acted on those different ideas. This illustration was a painful one to include but will be worth it if it brings home the criticality of leaders walking hand-in-hand in the same direction under the Lord's leadership.

Leader

Christ the King Community Church has a very organic model for growth. Their approach to leaders illustrates the foundational importance of having a leader for a site before moving.

Pastor Dave Browning recounts, "A couple years ago, we got a little bit on our high horse and I put out a list of communities that we would like to get something started in. Then I repented of it. I came back to our leaders and said, 'Remember that list of communities?' I said, 'Forget that, because that is not how God is really moving in this story.'

"'Let's just pray for leaders. Let's do what Jesus told us to do. Let's pray for leaders to go out into the harvest. And let's support those leaders wherever they surface. It might be in an adjacent community, but it might be around the world.'" As Christ the King has been faithful in providing this support, leaders indeed have surfaced in other areas.

Christ the King puts great emphasis on God raising up new leaders in their organic model of replication. Browning explained, "When we have the leaders to start another ministry we will start it. So sometimes a group might be thirty-five people, but they launch another group of twenty people in a neighboring community. Size isn't really the factor. We feel like the time to multiply is when we have the leaders to do it."

Cedar Park is much more structured than Christ the King, yet they place a similar emphasis on the leader. They do not build an intentional plan and then try to find the pieces. "It's more partnering with people that God has called into pastoring. Or we are raising up people internally, and then we basically partner with them where they feel like they are called and where God is putting them."

The principle of having a leader for the campus in place before you move forward is exemplified in churches who utilize live teaching as well as those who use video teaching. Someone must be in place with dedicated time and responsibility to make things happen behind the scenes. They also must be visible and reachable as people at the new site need someone with whom to connect and be supported.

One of the few churches that did not have a campus pastor at the launch of their second site was Desert Vineyard. Pastor David Parker recalls, "Initially I was heavily involved with a core of people, kind of a committee of layleaders." However, as Parker reflects on advice for other churches considering multi-site, he immediately focuses on the leader. "The thing that I would do differently is I think that I would begin with that off-site pastor. I would want to have that as part of the beginning when we do it again, which we will!"

Core Group

The leader also is joined at the hip with the layleaders within the core group. The campus pastor motivates and empowers a core group of people to take ownership of the different aspects of the ministry.

Henderson Hills had been thinking about moving toward a multi-site model for a couple years. Then a church roughly an hour away approached them about becoming a multi-site campus of their church. God's movement in a core group signaled that it was time to start.

The core group's importance is raised by inherent characteristics of those the new site is trying to reach. "A lot of times when you are starting something new, people, in the very best way, just want to window shop and see what is going on," observed Owen Nease, campus pastor at Henderson Hills.

LifeWay Research surveyed a large group of the "formerly churched," those who attended church regularly for at least a year as an adult, but currently do not attend church. When asked how they might want to visit a church, they confirmed this preference for a window-shopping approach.

Only 11 percent said they would be willing to identify themselves as a visitor when visiting a church for the first time. The vast majority prefer to remain anonymous on a first visit to a church and may for several subsequent visits.

Nease applied this principle to starting a new site. "It is sometimes hard to move people from that point to the point of really diving in and volunteering and investing their life. So getting people to move to that point in a quick way, but at the same time not pushing them there too quickly has been a little bit of a challenge."

The Holy Spirit often works over a period of time in the hearts of unbelievers and formerly churched adults. You need a core group that can allow the church to thrive as you give these individuals time to develop spiritually.

Location

These six prerequisites overlap, so a location has no meaning or significance without people.

As you begin to ask yourself if God has provided you with a location, you need to primarily be talking about people. Ultimately location includes both the community you are intent upon reaching and the physical premises in which you will meet. In terms of a prerequisite, you only need to identify the community to which God is calling you. The physical premises can come later in the process.

Dave Lonsberry, executive director of business and finance at Christ Fellowship, voiced what many multi-site churches have demonstrated. "We are looking for how we can take the ministry of Christ Fellowship closer to where we already have a base of leadership in place. One of our primary factors in deciding where we are going is 'do we have a base of leadership and a solid foundation of people so we can have momentum quickly?'"

Joe Stowell, executive pastor at Harvest Bible Chapel, indicated that once you feel the Lord leading you to multi-site, "choosing where you are going to go is such a big choice. It doesn't sound very exciting, but there's a lot that goes into it. Obviously you are not going to add an extension campus five blocks from your old one. It's the same neighborhood."

Using their congregation's zip codes, Harvest looked at where people drive from to attend. They also looked at which communities were growing the fastest that they could reach. Seeking the Lord's leadership, they examined this data and were led to start a campus twenty miles to the west of their original campus.

The life cycle of neighborhoods that prompted many urban churches to relocate just a generation ago is now prompting suburban churches to realize they are now located in a mature or declining suburban neighborhood.

While many churches have success stories to tell of relocating their church from an urban to a suburban location, there is also a long list of missed ministry opportunities that occurred in these scenarios.

Several multi-site churches have reversed the trend from a generation ago by adding downtown sites. Cornerstone's Temecula campus meets in a movie theater in downtown Temecula, whereas their original campus is ten miles south of town. The fact that there were ninety thousand people in Temecula who weren't going to church prompted them to go back.

City Place is a trendy ten- to twelve-block area of downtown West Palm Beach. My wife, Debbie, and I visited City Place as we celebrated our tenth anniversary in the West Palm Beach area. I bought a souvenir T-shirt across from the Harriet Himmel Theatre and we enjoyed some great ice cream in a nearby plaza. What we didn't know was that just a few months earlier, Christ Fellowship had begun services in that theater as their third campus.

The developer had renovated a former church and created the Harriet Himmel Theatre. In the spring of 2005, Christ Fellowship signed a contract to begin a weekend service there for their college and young adults called Ascent. The following fall they added their first "Christ Fellowship" service there intended for all ages.

This campus now has three services totaling about a thousand in attendance. The building where they meet is a landmark at the heart of one of the most popular sections of West Palm. Christ Fellowship capitalized on a surge of new activity in the downtown of their city. Their location is noticeable, it is easy to give directions to, and is even along the path of more than a few tourists.

Systems and Structures in Place

A military offensive conveys the sense of movement and urgency that are not dissimilar to the launch of a new church site. Many military campaigns have been won or lost, not at the front line, but at the supply line.

As you begin to think about extending your church to another location, you are in essence extending your supply lines. The strength of those supply lines is critical to your success. In much the same way that military supply lines cannot move into place before the front-line soldiers, so you cannot implement all of the service and organizational changes necessary for multi-site prior to launching. However, serious preparations do need to be made in advance.

My favorite professor at Wharton was Scott Armstrong. What made him stand out was his fearlessness in challenging generally accepted business principles. For example, he pointed out the fallacy of using military and sports analogies in business. "The objective in both sports and war is to beat the competitor. Business, on the other hand, aims to create wealth." While sports and military examples apply to seeking to defeat sinful desires and the powers of darkness, there are many other aspects of the Christian life in which such analogies imply the wrong objective.

For this reason and because the best example of supply lines today does not exist with a military power, let's draw some insight from another very large organization, Wal-Mart.

Wal-Mart has an infrastructure in place that is and always has been a key to their success. Internally Wal-Mart pioneered inventory practices that lowered their costs much more rapidly than other retailers. They put systems in place to automatically reorder products as they sold. For bulky products like diapers, this saved on shelf space, storage space, and overall inventory cost. This dedication to innovation and discipline has allowed Wal-Mart to deliver to customers the low price promise that has attracted a volume of business greater than the GDP of 144 countries in 2006.[1]

In recent years Wal-Mart has moved beyond reacting quickly to actually anticipating demand. They even track the weather as a predictor of what customers will need. When they see a hurricane tracking toward the coast, they are already sending supply trucks with the bottled water and tarps that will be needed in the aftermath. Their proficiency in supplying and supporting their retail stores who carry out their mission gives us a taste for the importance of having good supply lines.

In the same way we encouraged you to assess the health of your church and the health of your leaders in chapter 1, it is also important to check the health of your services and organizational structure before you begin the multi-site journey.

Your organization must be clear and your processes must be functioning smoothly before you begin to make the myriad of changes required by adding sites. In other words, the administration of your church must be healthy or you will be multiplying futility.

Even successful multi-site churches are forced to hit the pause button when they get ahead of their infrastructure. Celebration Church has grown from one to five campuses since being founded in Jacksonville, Florida, in 1998. Pastor Stovall Weems recalled, "We have expanded very fast, very quickly. And the negative to that is that we have not had, to this point, the adequate structures and systems for things to be as effective as they can. . . . We need to get everything really strong and strengthened with those necessary systems before we go and add a whole bunch more campuses."

Pastor Nathan Lewis of Evergreen Presbyterian Church also admitted, "We've done it all backwards." He recognizes that "it's been real messy organizationally" as the church, founded in Beaverton, Oregon, in 1993, has grown to three sites. While administration is not his strength, he recognizes that "the more that can be planned out and organized and micromanaged, is probably for the better." To this end, Evergreen recently added an executive pastor to their staff, much to Lewis's relief.

The difference between an inventor and an entrepreneur is that the entrepreneur has not only creative talent but also the ability to manage.

Central Services

Barry Galloway's background is in church planting. Today he serves as the campus pastor for the Tehachapi Mountain Vineyard campus of Desert Vineyard. "Being a church planter, I know the challenges of a young growing church are the same for probably every young growing church. The advantages of being a multi-site far outweigh the challenges, because you have all the resources of the Desert Vineyard to help you do things from just hard work to bulletins and the nuts and bolts of church."

The original church offers what many call "central services" to all of the sites. This creates efficiencies that are beneficial not only in the start-up phase but continuing afterwards, as well. The time and financial savings are easy to imagine. Time does not have to be invested in writing new employee policies or deciding employee benefits. The new site doesn't incur start-up expenses for purchasing accounting software or hiring accountants or bookkeepers.

While staffing for central services does eventually need to grow as the church grows, this personnel growth is much slower than if the services were replicated at each campus.

"Central services is kind of the tool shed for the entire network," says Dave Browning at Christ the King Community Church. "Central services gives a little bit of an administrative backbone to the entire network."

It follows that if central services is one of the practical benefits of multi-site, it is truly only a benefit if you have good central services. This includes having people in place who are skilled in areas such as purchasing, accounting, human resources, graphic design, and the like. This also means that processes are in place that make it clear how to request things, from whom, at what time.

If the senior pastor of your church is not gifted with administration skills, it is even more important to make sure there is someone on staff who can provide leadership in this area.

Barry Smith, senior pastor at Impact Community Church, describes both himself and most of his staff as "not very administrative." Impact soon learned that "there was really no one there to pick up the slack of all the enormous amount of administration and leadership details that it takes from the hospitality aspect, the signage aspect, and everything about planting a church."

Once your church has good services and organizational structures in place, you must change them.

That's right. When you add sites to your church, everything changes. However, it is always easier to adapt a process that works to multiple sites than to overhaul a process amidst all the other multi-site changes.

Ministry Staff

In addition to central services, there are also ministry organization questions that must soon be answered. Guidance on staffing can be found in chapter 9. The key question to answer as a prerequisite is: Are your church's ministries led by staff who can lead a multi-site ministry?

If you do not have the ministry personnel in place who can build a new team to lead at the new site, that site will suffer.

Dan Scates at LifeBridge pinpoints what it takes to be a successful staff member when a church goes to multi-site: "My honest take is multi-site exposes staff people who are not team builders. If the staff

> *My honest take is multi-site exposes staff people who are not team builders.*

person is a team builder and they build ministry around key leaders and team who actually take on ministry, then this is not a stretch. This is not a difficulty. If it's a staff member who predominantly performs ministry, then this becomes a very difficult task for them. To be successful at a site, they have to have a team leader and build a team of people that accomplish a ministry at each and every site."

Finances

It might go without saying that adding a site to your church is going to cost some money. However, when it comes to ministry we often prefer to ignore this obvious fact.

At the age of eleven, my family moved from Minneapolis to Philadelphia. My dad, who had taught accounting in a community college for seventeen years, became an accountant at the U.S. headquarters for WEC International, a nondenominational mission with missionaries serving in more than forty countries.

The reality was, my parents were full-time missionaries, which made me an MK (missionary kid). While this does not carry all of the stigma of being a PK (preacher's kid), it was awfully close.

As an MK in the U.S., I never had to experience the MK challenge of adjusting to American life and culture upon reentry. However, I did have to adjust to the common missionary challenge of not knowing whether you would have the money for basic necessities.

I never did get used to the taste of powdered milk. I didn't enjoy the unrelieved dandruff I had from using a bar of soap to wash my hair, because we didn't have shampoo.

I still have bittersweet memories of the first Christmas. Caring people from our home church in Columbia Heights, Minnesota, had sent a huge box of presents. Each contained something we really needed like paper towels or toilet paper. As much as we celebrated the provision of these basic needs, this eleven-year-old felt more than a little disappointment that the contents of the box didn't feel more like the big boxes of toys my grandmother had sent years earlier.

Thankfully our family only experienced a couple years of "thin" financial support. However, my outlook on things financial is still affected by it. While my age places me in Gen X, my experience prompts me to act more like my grandparents who felt the Great Depression.

I share this to let you know, I don't like talking about church finances any more than you. We love to speak of God's provision after the fact, but most of us who have lived in ministry have known the restlessness and even fear as we have waited for that provision.

The fact that money or the lack thereof is a test of faith is probably why God's timing with money is rarely on the same schedule as our thoughts.

As we talked with LifeBridge, a multi-site church in Colorado, they were experiencing such a period of waiting. They have a vision to start campuses in numerous surrounding communities. Dan Scates explained that they have already added two sites. "One is a year old and one is two years old. We try to have a six-month ramp-up before we launch the site. That's our goal. And so currently, just because of funding, we have not been able to ramp up our next site."

There is a lot of wisdom bound up in the attitude of the writer of Proverbs in saying, "Give me neither poverty nor wealth; feed me with the food I need. Otherwise, I might have too much and deny You, saying 'Who is the LORD?' or I might have nothing and steal, profaning the name of my God" (Prov. 30:8–9).

The experience of these multi-site churches is that they step out in faith in many ways, but as LifeBridge demonstrates they also are not reckless or naïve in terms of finances.

"You've got to have the funds," Mike Miller stated, "or you are going to collapse on them. And you are going to bring people in and then have to walk away, which I think, would be really unfortunate. So you have to have the funding."

You must plan and plan responsibly. But also watch for God to use finances to indicate His direction. Christ's Church was able to move from renting space in a high school to renting space in a Methodist church (Saturday night service), to purchasing land and moving into a new building over the course of about three years.

Jason Cullum described how that occurred financially: "You know, that's been one of those things that we look at now and go, 'How in the world did we do this?' God had a plan, and I know a lot of people say that, but we started out, honestly envisioning this as a storefront type of thing. This property became available, and we had some members of our church who stepped up and said, 'We're willing to help make this happen,' and made probably the largest gift I have ever been a part of in a church to make this possible."

The unforeseen generosity of some members whom God prompted to give allowed the church to purchase the land and only to finance the construction of the building. Christ's Church experienced what any leader would love to experience. Rather than being envious, we can join them in glorifying God knowing that in one way or another God will likely use finances to communicate His will for your multi-site journey.

Even in business, budgeting and forecasting revenue are difficult to do. The businesses that are best at this are typically businesses that are doing the same things in the same way for several budget cycles. Adding a site to your church is anything but business as usual.

The basic components of budgeting for a new site are similar to the budget process for your current campus. Each church's specific budget will reflect the impact of many of the decisions with which this book helps.

Budgeting for Expenses

1. *The cost of personnel.* The decisions about staffing the new site will be the biggest cost component to consider. Advice on staffing is found in chapter 9. The advice here is to have clear communication between your financial leader who is building the budget and the people making the

staffing decision. This needs to be a dialogue so that the financial person knows the latest decisions and the decision makers are making informed decisions based on the true cost of those decisions.

2. *The cost of the facility.* This includes the cost of the structure whether that is a one-time purchase, a monthly mortgage payment, or rent. It also often includes expenses for utilities and insurance. The type of facility you choose also could affect your staffing decisions in terms of custodial or maintenance workload as well.

3. *The cost of doing ministry.* Keep in mind, you likely will not start the new campus with all of the same ministries you currently have at your original campus. However, you should be able to estimate these expenses based on your current ministry model and budget expenses for the ministries you plan to offer.

Some ministry expenses that are part of the incremental cost of adding the site are included in existing budget line items. Every budget item in your existing budget should be thought through from the new perspective of being a multi-site church. For example, your central services will be printing more bulletins. The children's ministry will have more leaders to account for at their next training event. Staff will be turning in more mileage for reimbursement.

4. *One-time start-up expenses.* Significant up-front expenditures for equipment are often required by the worship ministry and the preschool and children's ministry. While their budgets may look similar to others today at your original campus, it is because they have made investments over time in critical infrastructure. Purchasing sound, lighting, and screens for worship as well as tables and cribs for children's ministry can add up in a hurry.

Start-up expenses will be among the hardest things to estimate. It is so easy to take for granted equipment and supplies that you currently use. It is easy to forget that you will often need "another one of those." Some of these expenses may even be temporary in nature, such as signs for a rented facility that you only plan to be in a short time. Others may be permanent expenditures such as chairs for a worship center that you can take with you when you move.

Because of the difficulty of anticipating all of the start-up costs, add some contingency money here to cover things for which you fail to account. Mike Brisson at Cornerstone Community Church reflected, "Yeah, it has been a challenge because it cost a lot more than we thought it would and we should know better because it always does. Everything you want to do costs more."

When you see the total cost, you will probably be taken aback. Barry Galloway, a campus pastor at Desert Vineyard, said, "I never ask how much money something is going to cost. I ask, 'How many people will it reach for Christ?'"While literally counting the cost is one of the foundational elements before moving into multi-site, Barry captures the heart of the matter: whether multi-site is for your church is not determined by the size of the financial challenge.

With each of the other five foundational elements, you should join God where He is at work. If He has not yet begun to work in the financial arena, take heed. He is trying to tell you something. His plan is either different in its timing or in its method.

Budgeting for Revenue

Budgeting for revenue from a new site is difficult because you do not know at what pace God will add new people to this fellowship. Yet you must make an estimate.

Community Presbyterian was careful to lay out a multiyear financial plan. They were conservative in their estimates. They did not give the new site credit for the giving of the original 100 people who would go there to establish it. Using only an estimate of new growth of people and giving, they estimated that the new site would require financial support for five years before breaking even on its own.

They debated whether to finance this investment through a loan or line of credit. Ultimately they chose to fund it through their operating budget—freeing up $350,000 the first year and $250,000 the second year. Admittedly, this put strain on other areas of the budget, but they were able to do it.

Using operating funds made it easier for people to question whether the investment was worth it as the site began slowly. However, as things picked up in year two, their expectation was that they would meet the five-year plan.

Community Presbyterian's approach (not including revenue from the core group sent to start the site) is correct from the standpoint of accurately calculating whether the investment in the new site is paid for by *incremental* growth.

The alternative is to consider all offerings at the new site to be part of the new site from day one. Similar to a church plant, they are sending the core group to this new work. This approach to budgeting means they must account for lower revenue at the original campus to account for the loss of giving from the core group who move to the new site.

Crossroads Community Church has sent out an average of seventy-five to eighty people (including both adults and children) from the original campus to each of the three campuses they started. Pastor Keith Boyer explained, "A lot of those people were very committed, already on board supporting God's work financially, and they just transferred that to the campus that they are now a part of." Crossroads raised money up front that does not have to be repaid by the new campus for start-up costs.

Crossroads applies the giving of the core group to that campus, so "once that campus is launched the anticipation and expectation is that the campus be self-supporting—meaning it covers whatever their expenditures are for an annual budget of running the facilities, [staff], and outreach."

As with most aspects of multi-site, there are different approaches to how you budget for offerings for the new site. You must decide which is best for your church. As you compare your estimation of offerings to expenses, the important thing is that you are intentionally and accurately counting the cost.

There are also options in how budgeting occurs once sites are established. Typical multi-site churches have one budget. Many multi-site churches allocate funds for each site within the budget. Responsibility for the site's budget is usually held by the campus pastor, but some items may be centralized within ministry or central service budgets (e.g., supplies, curriculum, etc.).

Keeping tabs on the balance sheets of new sites can be done short term or long term. Harvest Bible Chapel tries to keep monies separate that they have invested in sites that they refer to as "extensions." As these extensions begin to bring in more offerings than they have expenses, this money is used to start new extensions or hire new people.

Regardless of how the sites are tracked, most multi-site churches make strategic and financial decisions based on what is best for the entire church. In doing so, they may subsidize a ministry that is financially negative because they believe in the ministry or may direct funds to the most effective ministry as they are led.

Pieces That Need to Come Together

We often don't like "prerequisites." Prerequisite is another way of saying "you have to wait." In college, it means you can't take the interesting class until you take the prerequisite lecture hall, "nobody will ever use this" class.

At the dinner table it means my son has to eat his green beans if he wants any dessert.

There are summer days in which my daughter won't even ride her bike because she doesn't want to put on her helmet.

So you can skip the point of this chapter and jump into the "good stuff." Find out about life in a multi-site church and all that. Go straight to the 401 class! Eat your dessert first! Ride free!

The truth is there is no helmet law for going multi-site. However, there is a warning on the side of the box your bike comes in: traveling the multi-site journey unprepared could cause irreparable damage to your church!

Throughout this book you will see numerous examples of challenges and specific advice for avoiding or weathering those challenges. You will also find that many of those challenges relate to these six prerequisites. So the critical advice right here is: start by taking care of the prerequisites. Is God at work in these foundational areas of your church?

Knowing Who You Are
and What Matters

When I first began working at LifeWay, I would eat lunch each day in the break room on our floor. Different people would gather to eat depending on the day, but it was very common to be joined by a coworker named Jerry Wolverton.

Jerry could single-handedly lighten the mood of the lunch crowd with his quick wit and a new story almost every day. His stories came from his years as a pastor, an earlier tour of duty at the Baptist Sunday School Board managing the advertising department, and from growing up in Nashville (as with many growing cities, natives are hard to find).

In addition to full-length stories, Jerry also had numerous life observations that left you thinking. I remember one such observation Jerry shared one day: "I never preach a sermon longer than fifteen minutes—I am not good enough for people to want to listen longer than that."

The wisdom in that statement was both in his perception of people and his humility when assessing his own skills. Despite—or maybe because of—the years that separated us, I found Jerry very easy to listen to. Yet as good of a storyteller and mentor as he was, Jerry knew that great communicators are a rare breed.

Difficulty Identifying Your Church

Typically there are two sources of difficulty in determining who your church is: either you are not completely honest about what you see in the mirror or you don't know what you are looking for.

An Honest Look

Seeing your church through rose-colored glasses is not uncommon. In fact, it is a natural tendency that preserves the sanity of many pastors.

A couple of years ago we asked pastors about twenty different characteristics and ministries in their church. We asked them if each was a strength, weakness, or was on par with other churches their size.

You won't be surprised that there was an overall reluctance to indicate things were a weakness. Only two ministries were listed as a weakness by more than a third of pastors. In general, a reasonable number of pastors claimed ministries were a strength (only five ministries were listed as a strength by more than 40 percent of pastors). However, when it came to preaching, 59 percent of pastors indicated preaching at their church was a strength relative to other churches.

Clearly most of those pastors did not share Jerry's humility. We have a tendency to see ourselves as a little above average.

The best means of accurately describing your church is usually through the combined wisdom of a trusted group of leaders within your church. Several proverbs reveal the value of such counsel. "Plans fail when there is no counsel, but with many advisers they succeed" (Prov. 15:22). Leaders should covet such feedback. "Righteous lips are a king's delight, and he loves one who speaks honestly" (Prov. 16:13).

Pastors who have such a trusted group of leaders already know their value. These are leaders who can provide them with critical thinking rather than just telling them what they want to hear. Pastors, who don't have such a group, must invest in developing one. "Yes men" don't make an effective leadership team.

The critical thing is for you as a leader to take off the rose-colored glasses. Discuss your answers to the questions later in this chapter among your trusted leaders. Put some tension on each other's answers, so you can be confident that the answers that emerge can bear the weight of your future multi-site endeavors.

Now, as you take an honest look at your church, what are you looking for?

A Defined Search

One of the early concepts that first-generation multi-site churches discovered was the concept of a church's DNA. Most of the available advice on multi-site DNA focuses on how to transfer your DNA to your new sites, but this is a moot point if you don't know what your DNA is. After all, what is the definition of a church's DNA?

DNA is itself an analogy. It does a good job of communicating that something will get reproduced in your new sites. We must go beyond such a picture to some concrete principles to understand what is that "something" that needs to be transferred.

This is your church's "-IVE."

Identity: Who is your church?

Values: What matters to your church?

Expression: How does your church function?

-IVE is a suffix or word ending that means acting or inclined to act in a certain way. Have you articulated how your church is inclined to act? Have you specified how your church is designed to move?

-IVE often is found at the end of an adjective. You know when something is expens-IVE, it will cost a lot. You know that you will understand something better if it is descript-IVE. You are assured of something help-ful or something you will approve of if it is posit-IVE. -IVE provides predictability. With -IVE, you know that something will act a certain way. This assurance is what you are looking for at your new site(s) and throughout your church.

A well-articulated, well-tested -IVE will clearly and succinctly artic-ulate your church's identity, values, and expression. This acronym will help you take an honest and defined look at who your church is, what matters, and how you move.

Identity: Who Is Your Church?

In marketing, they call it "branding," but the Bible refers to it as one's name.

The Bible says a good name is to be chosen over great wealth (see Prov. 22:1) and is better than fine perfume (see Eccles. 7:1). One's name encompasses things like character, reputation, your roots, and what you stand for.

Your church's identity can be boiled down to two elements: its beliefs and its vision.

Beliefs

Beliefs are your roots, your foundation. Paul referred to the church of the living God as "the pillar and foundation of the truth" (1 Tim. 3:15). Like a foundation, your church's beliefs should be solid-ified and unchanging, whose chief cornerstone is Jesus Christ. With-out the foundation's firmness, a church cannot stand.

Vision

The second element of identity is your church's vision—what your church can see itself doing in the future. This vision reflects who God has gifted your church to be as well as the mission He has given you to do.

Articulating your church's identity is critical to maintaining, sustaining, and achieving it. If your church's beliefs, rooted in Scripture, are not written down and evident, then you will find different teaching arising within your church. If the future direction of the church is not clearly communicated and regularly repeated, well-meaning people will pull the church in different directions.

At the end of the day, everyone who comes to your church needs to be able to put into words what makes your church worth visiting. If they can't share where God is taking your church and what makes your church great between the parking lot and the front door, at work or the grocery store, they probably won't even try. If you as a leader can't say it succinctly, you can bet those who attend can't either.

Putting into words your church's identity is "positioning" your church appropriately in people's minds. You are positioning your church's beliefs compared to alternative belief systems or the diverse church backgrounds your attendees represent. You are positioning the destination(s) that your vision includes. Placing these stakes in the ground helps explain the steps your church takes toward them. Positioning also requires relating these beliefs and vision to the lives of those you meet.

There are certain elements of positioning that every Bible-believing Christian church will share in common. The key benefit we offer to people is communicating the opportunity available to everyone to have their relationship with the God of the universe restored through the saving work of Jesus Christ (see John 17:20–23). Two other benefits every local church offers to believers is the opportunity to worship God together with other believers and to be instructed in how to walk with God and please God (see 1 Thess. 4:1).

If this is your church's general positioning, what is its specific positioning?

A rule of thumb about church life that Jerry Wolverton shared with me one day was that "there are three things that matter in a church: good preaching, good music, and a good Sunday school. You have to be really good at two out of the three to have a successful ministry, because you can keep positive momentum if one isn't great, but two negatives will overcome you."

Look past the labels he used and see the wisdom rooted in these words.

1. Communication, context, and community are still the building blocks of what makes a great church.
2. You don't have to be good at everything to be a successful church, but you need enough positives to overcome the noise of neutrality (or negatives) and to maintain movement.

Positioning is about helping people articulate the positive—associating your church with the movement God creates and biblical beliefs they espouse. This description will not only be something they want to talk about, it will be something that the people you are trying to reach want to hear.

Three multi-site churches clearly demonstrate specific positioning. Who the church is emerged moments into the interview and permeated the entire conversation. Clearly they knew who they were and it kept them focused through the myriad of decisions required as they extended this identity to new sites.

Healing Place Church

In 1993 Dino and DeLynn Rizzo started a church in Baton Rouge, Louisiana, with about twelve people. As with most church plants, outreach was a priority from the beginning. Marc Cleary and Dan Ohlerking on Healing Place's lead pastor team explained, "Our whole approach to doing ministry has been outreach straight up, all the way.

"It started out as Trinity Christian Center. The subtitle or slogan, the motto, the mission of the church has always been, 'A healing place for a hurting world.' In 2000 we changed the name of the church . . . Healing

Place Church hits the nail on the head. It has always been outreach to the poor and hurting. It has been the mission God gave us right off the bat."

Even when the church had few people and few monetary resources, they demonstrated this identity. "One day a pastor cut the grass and had nothing else on the agenda for the day, so he went and bought a bunch of flowers and visited widows. That is the mind-set: 'Just find what you can do. Everybody can do something.'

"From there it has grown. That mind-set is still the same heart. We have more capacity because there are more people, more resources. But it's still the same: 'Let's find what nobody else wants to do and find the people that nobody else wants to serve, and let's serve them.'"

Healing Place does multi-site differently than many other multi-site churches. Their expression came from a clear understanding of their mission, their values, and the people they were trying to reach. They applied this understanding to the common decisions that every multi-site church must make.

Peppered throughout their story, Cleary and Ohlerking communicated a specific positioning for their church. "We are a church who cares about the community, who shows the love of Christ in every situation. That's kind of our reputation, our flow."

As we walk through the key decisions in moving to multi-site, you can follow this same course. Understand who you are and the vision God has given to your church. Then apply that understanding to each decision.

Northland, A Church Distributed

I have to admit that Northland's full name gave me a false expectation about their specific positioning. I simply thought "A Church Distributed" was a way to position their church around the attribute that their church is a multi-site church. However, as we stated in the first chapter, all of the multi-site churches we studied did not see being multi-site as an end. It was simply a tool.

This is true of Northland as well. Tim Tracey, executive director of worship, explained, "Our mission is to connect with other churches and to worship God and to serve one another. The multi-site model becomes a vehicle by which to do that."

The term *church distributed* reflects a conscious decision Northland made in 1998. They chose to center their church on relationships, rather than on a physical church building. As if this were not a big enough move, they also extended their concept of relationships to include not only relationships within the church but also relationships with partner ministries and their people distributing their lives every day in ministry to others.

The way Northland uses their sites stems from their identity. Tracey explained the reason Northland moved to multi-site "primarily grew out of a centrality of worship that Northland has always centered its entire ministry around—our highest and most glorious calling and our focus on this earth is to worship God."

Worship is the first of Northland's core values, and it is an integral part of their vision and mission. As they considered how they would do multi-site, the centrality of worship brought them to a practical conclusion. "If we are going to be together, we're going to be together in worship," Tracey explained. This has expressed itself in concurrent worship. Across their sites worship occurs at exactly the same time and is linked via two-way video that allows real-time interaction among sites. "Everything is concurrent—at the same time. Everybody on the same book and page in every location all the time," Tracey described.

Northland made decisions about how they would deliver the message, how similar the sites would be based on their identity. While this clear understanding of who they are as a church made some decisions easy, it did not mean the work of making it happen is easy. In fact, you cannot get much more complex than concurrent worship. "We are talking about something that no one else is doing. It's very hard," Tracey admitted. "Now I know why no one else has touched it."

North Point Community Church

North Point's identity revolves around the group of people they are trying to reach: young adults. Director of North Point Ministries David McDaniel doesn't apologize for having a narrow focus for their outreach. "There's just a certain audience that we're probably going to appeal to and you know what? There's so many lost people that fit that demographic that we're not going to try and broaden."

McDaniel puts this focus in perspective. "It would be arrogant for us to think that we need to go reach those other cultures when God can raise up leaders to do that. We've got more than we can reach that are just right here under our own noses."

This focus on a narrow age demographic transformed the development of both their approach to ministry and their decisions as they began to add sites.

For example, decisions about the music used in worship went back to this target group. McDaniel explained, "We try to use culture as a way to get people into the service. And so we're playing music that is more edgy than even a typical contemporary kind of service. We're really trying to aim it toward twenty-eight- to thirty-year-old males, typically." Because North Point sees this narrow group's musical taste is similar across the country, they play the same kind of music at all their locations.

In the same way, North Point's choice of locations for their sites focused on areas with high concentrations of twenty-five- to forty-four-year-old college educated folk.

As you consider practical aspects of multi-site, and as you move through the decisions in this book, you will need a firm grasp of your church's identity.

For churches, specific positioning will most often be focused on one of three things:

1. an attribute (although being the "first" Baptist church or the largest church in town is often less effective than other positionings)

2. a benefit

3. a specific audience

The Healing Place has clearly positioned their church on the benefit of helping people at their point of need. Northland has positioned their church on the benefit of worship on a grand scale across multiple locations—even churches in foreign countries on occasion. North Point's identity revolves around a specific audience they are trying to reach: young adults.

Each of these churches has other strengths, but they have kept their specific positioning succinct and as focused on their core identity as possible.

Below are some questions to help you evaluate your church's specific positioning. Attempt to answer each question reflecting God's activity in your church.

- What words do people use frequently to describe your church?
- What attributes, programs, or characteristics is your church known for?
- Whom has God called your church to reach?
- What stories do people tell about your church?
- Is there a common thread as to the types of changes God brings in people's lives through your church?
- If your church were a person, what positive personality traits would you say your church exhibits?
- Does your church have a tag line? Do people use it?

Values: What Matters to Your Church?

In addition to clearly articulating who your church is, you must also spell out the values that your church holds closely. This anchored and shared focus will help tremendously as you decide what your church will transfer to each site.

Eric Geiger, coauthor of *Simple Church* and executive pastor at Christ Fellowship Church, exhibits having clear ministry processes in place. Not only does Christ Fellowship have clearly articulated values; these values are the basis of staff evaluations. This is a clear example of the old saying that an organization values the things that are measured.

Stovall Weems, lead pastor at Celebration Church, points out, "It's that principle of saying yes to one thing and saying no to something else. The opportunity of multi-site is it helps you focus on what your mission and your values are."

Once you have articulated your church's identity—who you are and the mission God has given you—you must decide what is mission critical.

The fact that a fool repeats his folly (see Prov. 26:11) can be extended to define two other types of people. Ordinary people learn from their mistakes, but a truly wise man learns from the mistakes of others.

Several multi-site churches failed to apply their values to decisions related to their new sites and suffered for it. As with any of the negative illustrations, I share this not to embarrass or disparage, but to allow other churches to avoid these same mistakes. For that reason, I won't name the church in this first example.

> *It's that principle of saying yes to one thing and saying no to something else.*

Missing Values

This church had a site that was not able to continue. The pastor described worship as the strength of their church. Although admitting that it might sound bad, the pastor described their church as "worship driven." They ran into problems at this new site when the music and singing in worship did not measure up to the caliber of their original site. In hindsight, the pastor realized, "That [worship] didn't fit our model. And so it suffered."

As North Coast Church launched their second and third campuses, they allowed existing small groups to continue even though members would be worshipping at different locations. Pastor Larry Osborne identified the problem this caused. "It's not a deal killer for us, but we realized later when you shoot off a church, it's better if your people are seeing the friends from their small group rather than half of them being at the other campus. It just creates a more relationally connected church. So it's not like one fails and one succeeds; it's just one is way better.

"Here's one of the ways we noticed it: the buzz factor," Osborne continued. "On our campuses that started as off-loads, when you show up, there's not the same relational buzz going on as there is on the ones that have all their small groups tied to that campus. For us that's real noticeable, because we're a church built around small groups. Eighty percent of our weekend attendance is in a small group. People who visit our church are always amazed at just the energy in the plaza. It's really not anything we've created. It's because we're a big church and we have lots and lots of relationships. Of course that wasn't as consistent when we planned another venue out there and only half of the people were there from their group.

"As people gather for worship at a site, you have the typical conversation: 'Hi, how you doing?' Well, we cut that in half, which wasn't our smartest move."

Applied Values

A couple more examples that don't revolve around mistakes were two churches who intentionally focused on things they valued as they shaped their new sites.

Dan Scates, whose pastor, Rick Rusaw, coauthored the book *The Externally Focused Church*, stressed the importance of knowing the mission and purpose of the additional site and to determine what you call a successful site. He described these for LifeBridge: "We've got two main things we are trying to create: a community of people in the towns around us to worship together and grow together; and then we're also trying to create our external focused evangelistic ministry in that community from those people. When those two things are accomplished, we feel like we're successful."

Pastor Dave Browning demonstrates the importance of multiplication in how Christ the King Community Church views success. "Growing to a large size does not necessarily get rewarded. I mean, it's great if it happens, but that's not the goal. We don't think bigger is better. We think more is better. So we're always trying to find more leaders and more opportunities where we can start new ministries."

The anonymous church above clearly valued worship. The "hub" of North Coast is their small groups. LifeBridge values externally focused ministry, and Christ the King values multiplication.

Each of these churches has articulated values that inform their decisions. We have highlighted some of the more visible examples of values. Other less visible values may be things like valuing fun, flexibility, or creativity. These communicate that the way things are done matters to your church.

Below are some questions to help you evaluate your church's values. Attempt to answer each question reflecting God's activity in your church.

- What makes the culture of your church distinctive?
- What does your church celebrate or get most excited about?
- How does your church define success?
- What element, when missing, leaves a church activity feeling empty?
- What does your church look for within candidates as you hire new ministers?
- What are the important things that are communicated to those wanting to get involved in your church?
- Does your church have a written list of values? Are those the things people in the church really value?

Olathe Bible Church was a multi-site church for a number of years before they finally answered these questions. As they saw their own reactions to certain decisions in the multi-site process, they realized their heart was really in church planting. The signals included not wanting to staff an additional layer of ministers to oversee ministries across campuses and valuing a large degree of evangelistic autonomy at the sites to reach people they considered quite different from their original site. Lead pastor Mike Bickley explained the staffing issue. "We really struggled to *not* be a staff-led church, but an elder-led church. We found multi-site, which takes a ton of staff involvement, to be a hard reality for us."

Clearly many multi-site churches have elder oversight and many also plant churches. In fact, more often than not Olathe could technically count as a multi-site church. However, they have clarified their vision for the new sites to be planted and autonomous as they become healthy in leadership development, evangelism, ministry, and finances. Bickley shared Olathe's perspective: "We have seen it more like parenting. They're in our house for a period of time, but our whole goal is to send them out."

This realization of what the staff and members really value has energized their church planting. "The multi-site experience really did help clarify who we are and where we are going and 'Will this fit?' I would tell people we failed at being a successful multi-site church. And that failure led us to be very successful in several church plants. So we see that foray and that failure brought about what God desired all along for our particular body."

Woodcrest Chapel's journey into multi-site is a mirror image of Olathe's journey out of multi-site. Woodcrest had agreed to be a consultant for a new church thirty-five miles away in Jefferson City. Their pastor also agreed to commute and preach on Sunday evenings when they met. After about a year, the leadership of the fledgling church approached Woodcrest Chapel about the possibility of actually being incorporated under the umbrella officially of Woodcrest Chapel. The leaders of the church plant felt that they could not go where they had hoped to go on their own.

As Woodcrest Chapel began to invest in the Jefferson City location, they also realized multi-site was a solution for their landlocked Columbia location. Soon multi-site was part of their identity and a tool to accomplish their vision. Tim Davis, guest relations and multi-site director, summarized this vision. "Our vision is to be able to take this approach to ministry to the surrounding smaller communities and to be able to go into these communities with a quality presentation of the gospel in a refreshing way, in a way that speaks truth in the language of the culture."

Expression: How Does Your Church Function?

Your church's identity and your church's values should rarely move, but the expressions of your church will change over time. They must change. Your beliefs should be rock solid. Your vision will change once or twice in your lifetime. Your values should only be nuanced through the years. But the expressions of your church will need to change to reach new generations, to help believers remain externally focused, and to become more effective.

Identity is who you are. Values are what matters to your church. Expression is how your church functions. The basic elements of worship, evangelism, discipleship, fellowship, ministry, and prayer should be present in every local church, yet their expression varies. These expressions are greatly impacted by the identity and values of your church, but they should also be strategically guided.

Intentional Process

The activities of your church include specific actions, events, and programs. These activities tend to multiply and can easily be consuming.

"Perhaps we are losing ground not *despite* our overabundance of activity but *because* of it," Thom Rainer and Eric Geiger observed in their book *Simple Church*.[2] They went on to appeal to churches to have "a straightforward and strategic process that moves people through the stages of spiritual growth."[3]

This type of intentional ministry process is the predictable part of expression. The activities that are placed in the process will change names, times, leaders, and locations over time. However, the process provides stability in how your church functions that must be replicated at your new sites.

Process Improvement

Over time your church improves the way it does things. This incremental learning helps things flow more smoothly and become more effective. This learning is not what really matters to your church, but it does allow your church to do the important things better.

Finding better ways of doing things is ongoing. By sharing this learning and establishing best practices, your church focuses its energy on new challenges. Once your church articulates these best practices, it will need to continually assess if you are functioning at that level. Joe Stowell, a teaching pastor at Harvest Bible Chapel, calls it "quality control. We have a certain level of what we want to do at worship and children's ministry, and signage, etc. A person has to kind of walk around to be sure, evaluating that this all passes muster."

The following chapters will help you make practical decisions about specific expressions of your church as it moves to multiple sites. But first, give some thought to the questions below that help you evaluate the more predictable elements of your church's expression. Attempt to answer each question reflecting God's activity in your church.

- What is your church's ministry process?
- Which functions are primary and which are secondary in this process?
- What are the practices that have worked best in each of your areas of ministry?
- Why have these methods been effective?

If you realize your values need to change or that your church is not living out your stated values or lacks a ministry process, hit the pause button. Multi-site is not a parachute from problems with your current flight pattern.

McDaniel warned churches who are interested in multi-site because they want to get away from some older methods or programs or styles. "Really what you're doing is saying your old model is sick and you're trying to solve it by going multi-site with a new model that's new and different. I just think that is a recipe for disaster."

If something about who your church is—your identity, your values, or fundamental aspects of your expression—needs to change, fix it before you move to multi-site. This is important for two reasons:

First, it is virtually impossible to multiply something that does not exist in the first place. If your church isn't there today, you won't have the skill set, the experience, and the culture you need at your new site to draw upon in creating the new thing you have in mind.

> *If something about who your church is needs to change, fix it before you move to multi-site.*

Second, this type of fundamental change to who your church is will take work to get the necessary buy-in from your church. Moving to multi-site requires unity. There are too many changes occurring to try to change your -IVE at the same time.

This first section has allowed you to check your motives for wanting to become a multi-site church, helped you examine where God is equipping your church in fundamental multi-site prerequisites, and assisted you in articulating and testing how your church acts and is inclined to act—your -IVE.

Now you are ready to transition into planning your venture into multi-site.

**CHAPTER
FOUR**

Decisions That Define Your Multi-Site Church

D ave Ferguson, lead pastor of Community Christian Church, has been on the leading edge of the multi-site movement and has helped scores of other churches move into multi-site through the NewThing Network (www.newthing.org). He shares what he has come to see as the seven most important questions when going multi-site.

Dave Ferguson

lead pastor, Community Christian Church

It made me laugh when *Mental Floss* magazine strained their editorial brains to list "The 25 Most Important Questions in the History of the Universe." The list included hard questions that really matter like:

- "What makes No. 2 pencils so darn special?"
- "Who's that AOL guy who eerily knows when you've got mail?"
- "How can I win at that ultra-important-corporate-decision-making-process, rock-paper-scissor?"

While *Mental Floss* (whose slogan is "Where Knowledge Junkies Get Their Fix") may list those among the most important questions, there are other questions that are most important when it comes to multi-site. If you are among the growing numbers of churches that are considering reproducing through multiple locations, here are the seven most important questions you need to answer:

1. Dream Question: "What is the dream?"

One of the first questions I ask people when they tell me they want to go to multiple sites is, "How many sites?" or "How big is your dream?" If they say, "We'd like to be a church of two or three sites," then the answers to the rest of these questions are pretty simple and straightforward. Now, if they say, "We want to be a church of four or more sites," then the answer to future questions are more challenging. If the dream is ten or more sites, then you have to answer the remaining questions thinking about systems and continual reproduction.

One of the guys who has pushed me to dream bigger is Lyle Schaller. I love that old guy! Over and over he will rib me by looking me in the eye and saying, "Dave, your biggest problem is that I have a bigger dream for your church than you do!" And every time he says that, my dream gets bigger! Right now I'm dreaming of a church with two hundred sites locally and one hundred thousand 3C Christ Followers! And that doesn't include NewThing—that's another dream! Some of you reading this right now, your biggest problem is that God has a bigger dream for your church than you do! So start by prayerfully answering the question: "What is the dream?"

2. Brand Question: "What is essential to your brand?"

When McDonalds opens a new location, they may or may not have a playland, but you know they will have hamburgers. When Starbucks opens up a new store, they may or may not have a drive-thru, but you know they will have coffee. There are some things that are essential to a brand while things are optional. One of the tough decisions every church has to make when reproducing sites is determining which ministries are essential and which ministries are optional.

When Community starts a new site, we know that a celebration service, adult small groups, Kids' City, and hospitality are essential. At some of our larger sites we have a support and recovery ministry and a School for the Arts. I love our support and recovery ministry and School for the Arts, but we cannot afford to reproduce everything we do at our most established sites at our brand-new sites. So an important question is "What is essential to your brand?"

3. Organization Question: "What is your organizational design?"

If you answered the dream question by saying two or three sites, I would recommend an organizational design that takes your existing vertical ministry silos and adds a horizontal process across these ministries. The horizontal silos represent each campus. In this organizational design, the authority resides in the vertical silos and influence resides with the campus pastor in the horizontal silos. The organizational design looks like Figure 1 on the next page.

If you answered the dream question by saying four or more sites, I would recommend that you take the previous organizational design and turn it on its side. The biggest change is that the authority now resides with the campus pastor and the influence resides with the ministries. This is a necessary shift in order to make sure that effective ministry is happening in every context. The organizational design looks like Figure 2 on the next page.

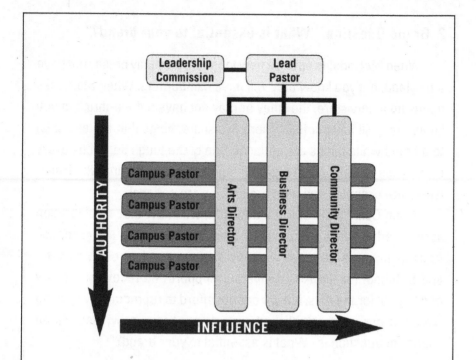

Figure 1: Organization for two to three sites

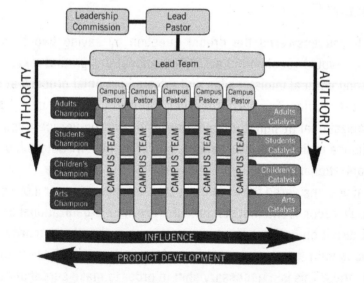

Figure 2: Organization for four or more sites

This is a critical question for churches that dream of more than four sites. If you don't answer this question, you will most likely not realize your dream.

4. Leadership Question: "Do you have a leadership farm system?"

Multi-site churches are like baseball teams. Baseball teams need a continual pipeline of new and young players who can take the field to improve their team and replace retiring players. These new players will come via free agency or through their farm system. The more expensive way is to pay big bucks and sign a free agent from another team. The more efficient means is to create a farm system that is constantly developing talent from within your organization.

Since a multi-site church's dream is to reproduce new sites, like a baseball team, it creates the need for a farm system of new and young leaders to fill ministry roles. Yes, a church can go the free agent route and recruit leaders from other churches, but churches with big dreams will never see them fulfilled if they are dependent on other churches and organizations to do their leadership development for them.

The churches that have created a farm system for developing more and better leaders usually do it through their small group ministry. At Community we have several campus pastors, and with our NewThing Network we have several church planters who have come up through the following farm system:

Figure 3: Leadership Farm System

Do you have a farm system that is growing up campus pastors? Where are you going to find the leaders and staff for those sites of which you are dreaming?

5. Artist Question: "Do you have a plan for artist development?"

Of all the multi-site questions on this list, the one that most often gets overlooked is the artist question. In the same way that you need a leadership development strategy, you also need an artist development strategy. Reproducing a new site can be looked at as simply reproducing all of your small group events and all of your large group events. And all of your large group events require artists who will facilitate and lead the worship services. These artists include those whom we see up front like musicians, vocalists, actors, and dancers, as well as those who are behind the scenes like sound technicians and videographers.

Because our dream is so big at Community, we have both an informal and a formal process for developing more and better artists. Our informal process is through apprenticeships. We encourage our actors to have an understudy, our musicians to second chair, and our technicians to have people shadow them. Our formal process is through our School for the Arts where we have more than four hundred artists enrolled in classes and workshops, developing and growing in their art.

If you are planning on reproducing more locations, what are your formal and informal processes for developing more and better artists?

6. Funding Question: "Is your funding in place?"

At Community we have nine locations. The campus launches that have gone the smoothest and been the most enjoyable had this question answered. The launches that have been the most challenging did not have this question answered. So before you start that new site, make sure you do some number crunching and know for sure that you have the funding in place.

The amount of funding this new site will need is different based on expectations and context. Some megachurches expect a new site to have more than a thousand in attendance at the launch and grow from there. These new sites will have budgets well over a million dollars. Other churches will start new sites with a single volunteer leader and will do it on a "shoestring." Chances are your church is somewhere in between. The best way to answer the funding question is to do the following:

1. Prepare a pro forma for the first three years of the new site.

2. Know and communicate the date you expect the site to be self-supporting.
3. Make sure you have secured all the funding needed for the prelaunch phase.

Make sure you answer the funding question. Failure to answer this question will not only impact the new site, but the existing church.

7. Alignment Question: "How are you going to maintain alignment?"

When we made the decision to go to multiple sites, Lyle Schaller gave me this prediction: "Dave, there will be lots of churches that will go to two sites, almost no churches with three sites, and lots more that will reproduce to four and beyond." And ten years later he was right. Why would this be true? Some churches answered the alignment question and others did not.

The alignment question wants to know how you are going to keep all the sites moving toward the same vision with the same values. If there is vision and value drift by any of the locations, it will slow down the whole church. But if you get all locations moving toward the same vision with the same values, you will exponentially increase the impact your church can make! Some churches with a big dream have stopped at two locations because they didn't answer the alignment question. Other churches are seeing their big dream realized as all their sites are moving forward in-step and having a huge impact.

At Community we have developed what we call "The Four 1's" that keep us in alignment:

- 1 Vision: every site is pursuing the same vision.
- 1 BIG IDEA: every site is being taught the same BIG IDEA.
- 1 Budget: we have multiple locations, but one church budget.

- 1 Eldership: we have a plurality of elders that represent all sites and oversee the church.

If your dream is more than two locations, answering the alignment question is critical!

If you want to be successful in your multi-site transition, make sure you answer these most important questions. And if these questions have scared you off, then maybe it will make you smile knowing that Elwood Edwards is the man behind the AOL message that sixty-three million times a day says, "You've got mail."

Throughout your journey, these seven questions will prove their importance. Now, as you are beginning to plan your multi-site venture, you probably already have some ideas. However, some decisions serve as building blocks that need to be in place to shape the rest of your plan. We will look at four of these decisions.

Four Decisions to Make Up Front

Decision: What level of autonomy will the sites have?

"We have seen different models," said campus pastor Owen Nease. "We have seen a model that is almost like a clone model, where campuses are very much directed by the primary campus. And we have seen other models where there is a lot more freedom in the multi-site locations. They get general direction from the primary campus, but they pretty much do their own thing."

However, seeing is different from deciding. Henderson Hills Baptist Church did not think through this structure prior to their Stillwater launch, and it created some confusion and "hiccups."

Chuck Carter, pastor of First Baptist Windermere, echoed this advice. "Get to know the different models that are out there, and let God lead you on what is going to best fit your church, your culture, and your people."

Dave Browning describes Christ the King Community Church's structure.

> We call our model a "centered set model" as opposed to a
> "bounded set model." And by "centered set" we mean there is
> a dot on the paper and that is our mission, vision, and values.
> And if you are drawn to that dot, to that mission, vision, and
> values, then you are pulling or going toward the center of this.
> A bounded set is more like you draw a big circle on a piece
> of paper and in order to get into the set you have to cross the
> boundary of that circle line into the middle. We don't have a
> boundary like that.
>
> We do have some variation. In an organic system we think
> there is both repetition and revelation. The repetition would
> be, you look at your kids and you say, "Wow, they kind of look
> like us." But then you also look at your kids and you say, "Boy,
> they really don't look like us too."
>
> I tell people, "If you have seen a Christ the King worship
> center, you have seen *one* Christ the King worship center,"
> because there is quite a bit of variation in our story—partly
> because of the communities we are in. We draw different
> sorts of people into our story from the communities, and that
> makes our stories different. We have different language groups,
> different nationalities that are meeting as Christ the King
> Community Church. So there is a lot of variation, culturally,
> linguistically, and so forth. But we are all united with the same
> mission, vision, and values.

Chartwell Baptist Church is another church that gives their sites a lot of autonomy. Jim Carrie, executive missions/outreach pastor, describes the objective: "We really want to empower each of our congregations to be fully congregational in that they have local decision-making rights and authority. We really want each congregation to have its own identity and yet still achieve success by working together."

An example of a more controlled model would be Harvest Bible Chapel, where consistency is valued. Teaching pastor Joe Stowell summarized: "A brand name is a brand name. We pretty tightly control logos, color schemes, and certain pantone colors they have to use. We call the children's ministry the same thing. They all get the same message every weekend."

Stowell's description of visiting Harvest Bible Chapel campuses is the opposite of the description Browning gave of Christ the King Community Church. Stowell says, "When people come to Harvest if you are from Chicago and you happen to be on vacation in Phoenix, it should feel very familiar. It should be same color, same logo, same bulletin. The children's ministry is even doing the correctly sequenced lesson."

Deciding how centralized versus decentralized or how uniform versus customized you want your sites to be does not have a "right" answer. However, the best advice for how to decide the appropriate level for your sites is sitting within your own church.

Guidance: Reflect your church's current leadership style.

Churches who gave their sites lots of autonomy were already organic churches who valued starting and trying new things. They simply applied this creative freedom to the new sites. Churches who had developed and valued refined processes and methods sought to apply this learning to the new sites. Trying to do something structurally different at the new site could quickly create an organizational culture clash.

Decision: Who will provide oversight to the multi-site effort?

Dan Scates, multi-site minister at LifeBridge, points out, "There are multiple decisions, lots of conflicts, lots of ways that the values that you have are challenged. You have to prioritize those values and make significant calls. Who really is going to be the key executive staff level person that's going to be over this and help it get somewhere? It's bigger than just a department in a church. It's really something that is an umbrella that covers all the departments."

Guidance: Oversight of multi-site work must be at the senior leadership level.

The next chapter will help you answer "who will lead the site?" The key decision that must be made at this point is "who at the executive leadership level of your church will be responsible for the site?" In other words, who will the leader of the site be accountable to? And as you add sites, who is going to lead the coordination of this effort?

Multi-site churches take one of two approaches:

1. Churches like Windermere Ministries and Desert Vineyard Christian Fellowship include the campus ministers on their senior leadership team.
2. Churches who do not put the campus minister at this high a level organizationally need to have a point person on that leadership team to steer the direction of the multi-site effort and to obtain direction or clarity from this senior team as needed.

Decision: How are you going to deliver the message?

The earlier you can decide this, the better. This affects the type of campus pastor you will hire. It affects the up-front cost of technology. It affects the expectations of staff and significantly changes the "to-do" list as you prepare.

There are numerous options:

- Live teaching at each site
  - » Fewer teaching pastors than sites with the pastor(s) traveling between sites
  - » A teaching pastor at each site who is also the campus pastor

- » A teaching pastor at each site plus a campus pastor
- » A team of teaching pastors who rotate between sites
- Video teaching at some sites
  - » Video delivered as live feed
    - ¤ Video teaching delivered and shown in real time (a live feed)
    - ¤ Video teaching delivered in real time but played when ready (a live feed with TIVO capability)
  - » Video delivered as DVD or stored file
    - ¤ Video teaching recorded on DVD and delivered to other sites unedited
    - ¤ Video teaching recorded on DVD, edited, and delivered to other sites
    - ¤ Video teaching played the same weekend it is recorded
    - ¤ Video teaching played a week (or more) after it is recorded
  - » Live teaching at only one service
  - » Live teaching at multiple services
  - » Recording done at one site
  - » Recording capability at multiple sites
    - ¤ One recording site used per service
    - ¤ Simultaneous recording and real-time delivery of video from multiple sites to multiple sites
  - » One teaching pastor used on video
  - » A teaching team taking turns on video

Clearly there are a growing number of options for the delivery of teaching to multiple sites. Most multi-site churches are advocates for the method they have chosen but are also quick to point out that their approach won't be right for every church.

The following examples of how churches deliver the message and insights they offer into why that decision made sense at their church should provide you with insight into how to look at what God is doing in your church that would impact this decision.

Examples of Video Teaching

Dan Scates indicated there were several reasons why LifeBridge chose to use DVD. "One, we do have a good speaker. Two, we do have some people who have some skill and ability in recording and taking care of the DVD. We felt like we could multiply this out many times over through that means. We felt like we could more easily recruit and train internal leaders to be campus pastors, instead of external. So, we felt like we could at a more rapid pace go hit five, six, seven, eight communities."

Christ's Church had to change their approach to teaching in the first site they added. They originally went with video at this site. The sixty-five to seventy families that formed the core group were used to the live teaching at Christ's Church without any image magnification.

Jason Cullum explained, "I would say it was probably more of a struggle for our people to get used to that than it was necessarily for new people coming in because it was something that was an expectation that they already had based on the fact that they had been used to our campus, our style of ministry, and what we had done."

Cullum advised those planning on using video in multi-site, "Do your best in your current services to go to image magnification and get people used to watching and seeing things on the screen and used to seeing the preacher preach on the screen, used to seeing some of the worship done on the screen."

Cornerstone Community Church has two big screens at their original campus and many people watch those instead of the platform, so they had no resistance from their core group to video teaching. Associate pastor Mike Brisson explained, "I don't think new people would say anything, they just wouldn't come back, so we didn't advertise that it was a video venue in outside advertising. It could be that people didn't choose to stick with us because we are a video venue, but I haven't read any cards or any feedback, gotten anything e-mailed or phone calls telling [us] that, 'Yeah, we are not going to stay here because it is not a live sermon.'"

Larry Ali, executive pastor at Desert Vineyard, describes their senior pastor, David Parker. "He has a unique gift to speak to both churched people and nonchurched people." Desert Vineyard's original campus has five thousand people, "so he is a gifted speaker. To have that speaker in a small town on video is not any sort of a distraction for people. To have this speaker in a small community, that's a great draw!"

"I don't think Joe Blow could do a video church. The preaching has to be excellent," says Barry Galloway, campus pastor at Desert Vineyard.

> *"I don't think Joe Blow could do a video church. The preaching has to be excellent," says Barry Galloway, campus pastor at Desert Vineyard.*

Taking this honest look at what you have in your hand can help you come to a decision. Cornerstone Community Church didn't get stuck on the philosophical side of this decision when they went to start their first new site. Mike Brisson explained, "We didn't have a man that wanted to step forward and speak every weekend and be the leader. That is why we chose to go with the video."

Notice some recurring principles:

- Video teaching works well when you have a great teaching pastor.
- Video teaching works well when God has gifted your church with people with the necessary technical and production skills.
- Video teaching works well when the core group of people who will launch the campus are used to seeing the primary teacher on a screen (image magnification).

Examples of Live Teaching

Windermere Ministries chose to have live teaching on all of their campuses. Two values drove this decision. "One of our values is options. So, we have live preaching at all our sites and different worship styles. What we have found is we have a much higher retention rate because we have given people options."

They also value the benefits of coming together to plan the direction of the church and for sermons. "Monday morning, the campus pastors, the executive pastor, and the business administrator come together. We plan. We dig ideas together about what we are to preach on in the next three months. We're preaching the same topic, but we put our own personality into it."

Although they value live teaching at each campus for these reasons, they are not opposed to using video as an additional venue. In fact, they recently added a video venue at their First Baptist Windermere campus.

Chartwell Baptist Church doesn't mandate that their pastors work together on teaching, yet "that is actually an asset for the church," noted Carrie. "Because we are multi-site, because we agree to a common philosophy of ministry, our teaching pastors will continue to work together and to share ideas together and to argue things together because they value the relationship."

Spring Baptist Church launched a second campus with only one teaching pastor. Pastor Mark Estep preaches two services at the Spring campus, then is driven to the Klein campus where he preaches a third service. While this was a staffing necessity, Estep doesn't downplay the effect. "If a pastor is going to preach at both campuses, he has to understand how taxing it is going to be on him physically, because if you preach at one service, that's one thing. If you preach two, you go into the second already a little tired. It is sort of exponential in its nature. By the time you have preached your third service, you are very tired going into it."

Live teaching at all sites is typically either a value of the church going into multi-site or it is a necessity while a church has just two sites.

It is important to point out that your approach to teaching may differ for different sites. Healing Place Church began their multi-site journey with a video site two miles from their original campus, and they use multiple teachers across their other sites.

Yet, there is still a lot of continuity across sites, Marc Cleary and Dan Ohlerking noted. "What we do is we all follow the same sermon series. It is not necessarily the same message, because it's how God speaks it through each speaker as they speak. But it is the same title, same topic, same video bumper, same graphics, all that."

Examples of Rotating

Although Celebration Church uses video teaching, they do rotate worship leaders and associate pastors between campuses. Celebration Church values this fluidity. "We try to keep a degree of unpredictability," said their pastor, Stovall Weems. "We like to keep a degree of 'you never know what's coming around the corner.'" At Celebration Church, attendees cannot help but understand that the church is not about the leader.

Celebration Church tried a lot of different things before landing on this type of rotation. Weems explained, "We've landed by the kind of leader I am and the kind of church that we are. Our flow really is one church with multiple locations, so there has to be a whole lot of sharing. We don't like things to get isolated. We like everything with a one big pot type of mentality."

Typically when we talk about rotation, we are referring to the rotation of teaching pastors. Rotating pastors can lead to some unpredictability at the campuses. If the quality is not similar across teachers, this will lead to reluctance to invite guests when they do not know whether they have the A-level or B-level teacher that week. However, if the quality is similar, rotating teaching pastors can provide the one church mentality to which Weems referred.

Both the senior pastor, James MacDonald, and teaching pastor, Joe Stowell, taught several services live on a typical weekend at Harvest Bible Chapel's two largest campuses. However, there are sermon series in which only one of them taught. The smaller campuses always have video teaching while several services each week at the larger campuses use video.

Since their rotation involved both having teachers rotating as well as rotating between video and live teaching, Stowell pointed out that they would have noticed if people were stuck on live teaching. "You would think people would vote with their feet. Then all of a sudden people would figure it out and the video service would be empty and the live one would always be full. But it's not like that. I don't think people really care."

Oasis Church utilizes more teaching pastors in their rotation. Pastor Guy Melton explains, "We rotate our teaching pastors to the different locations. We don't have one pastor teaching all the time. We have three that are full-time preaching pastors, and then we have five others that are actually part time. Some of them are full time on our staff, but [preaching] is not their priority. And then some of them are lay pastors that either have a full-time career or they are retired from one.

"We are all on the same series. We do sermon series that are more topical for the most part. So everything is pretty much on the same page, but with very different personalities. . . . It's just like having a family. You're all the same blood, but you all look very different and your personalities are totally different."

A teaching team allows for collaboration in sermon preparation that raises the quality of teaching and should improve the integration of teaching with the other elements of the worship service. Dave Ferguson provides detailed guidance on the strengths of this concept and how to do it in his book *The Big Idea*.

Valley Bible Fellowship uses rotation and has utilized two primary teachers, senior pastor Ron Vietti and teaching pastor Jim Crews. VBF has had campuses in Bakersfield, California, and Las Vegas, Nevada, for several years in which Vietti or Crews preached live at most services despite the 270 miles separating the campuses. More recently VBF has added theater campuses in Visalia and Reno. Instead of both teachers preaching the same content on the same week, Vietti and Crews each choose half of the sermons in a series and concentrate on preparing those. They preach those two sermons in one live location and then they swap and preach the same two sermons in the other city. People attending hear different styles from Vietti (more of a preacher) and Crews (more of a teacher), and Vietti and Crews have maximized their study and preparation time by each preparing half of the sermons.

Decision: What core ministries will you offer?

Determining what core ministries you will have at launch is a critical decision. As with so many of the decisions related to multi-site, there is not a right or wrong way to do it. Yet there are common principles to guide you.

Four guidelines are:

1. stay focused on who your church is and who you are primarily trying to reach,
2. have a plan for rolling out programs,
3. communicate that plan, and
4. don't get pulled away from your focus.

Healing Place Church was surprised when they started a video campus two miles from their original campus. "We were expecting a more New York City type of feel to it—the real metropolitan, real coffee shop, young," Marc Cleary and Dan Ohlerking described, "but what we found was a lot of the older people would [attend] because we didn't have kid's church or nursery right off the bat. So it limited the audience that would go to those who didn't have kids."

This site was close enough that it functioned a lot like a venue, so this did not prove to be a problem. However, if this failure to consider the people being targeted had occurred at a typical new site further from the original church, it could have made the site ineffective.

Christ's Church learned by experience the value of having a plan for rolling out programs and communicating that plan. "The expectations were that they were going to have the same quality of programming, the same type of programming at that campus immediately. And the reality is we couldn't do it. There was no way we could possibly duplicate what we were doing here for a different type of venue with fewer resources and fewer people." As leadership realized there were some unmet expectations at the new site, they began to communicate, "There is a process to this. At this point we are going to be able to do only this."

Having a plan and maintaining focus are critical. Resources are often stretched as a site is launched, so beginning with too much programming or adding it too quickly can easily overload your core leadership. Many things that cannot be done with the same quality level that your church is known for should be delayed as well.

Expect pressure to add programs, ministries, and services faster than you can or should offer them. Nathan Lewis at Evergreen Presbyterian included this in his advice for those beginning the multi-site journey. "Don't jump too quickly when an individual, especially a visitor, mentions, 'What we're really looking for is such and such.'" Lewis indicated that in the early stages at a site, you need to respond by saying, "'We are just not ready to provide that program or service or ministry yet.' And don't jump in and think, 'Oh, I want this family to join us so I'm going to cook up something real quick to serve them.'"

Lewis advised, "Welcome them and let the Holy Spirit work on them whether or not they are to be called into that site or not, because I have seen ministry team members and especially church planters become quite anxious and then they throw something together sloppily and then, most of the time, the person who suggested it never comes anyway."

As Valley Bible Fellowship launched their Las Vegas site, they stayed focused on core ministries that mattered to their church such as small groups and ministry to the poor. However they moved within these ministries faster than they developed local leaders.

Senior pastor Ron Vietti explained, "We brought leaders over originally from the big church and they automatically thought the small church could do a large percentage of the things the big church was doing. They were trained in the big church. So we had all these Christianity groups, all these outreaches to the poor, and we had all these things going, and we didn't have enough people to facilitate them and we almost buried ourselves."

As ministries are added for the new site, it actually creates a choice for some core leaders and attendees who cannot add that to their current commitments. "So we have been very intentional to prefer certain things over others," said Dave Lonsberry, executive director of business and finance at Christ Fellowship Church. "We want to make sure that we just make the choice very clear for people in terms of what we would like to see them do."

A related question regarding what core ministries you are going to offer is, where will they be offered? What will be conducted at the new site and what will be only available on the original campus? Clearly, sites that are within driving distance can utilize more ministries of the original campus than sites that are distant. However, multi-site churches with sites that are within driving distance have come to different conclusions about how much to encourage attendance of activities at other sites.

North Coast Church in Vista, California, started their second and third sites within six to ten miles of their original campus. They did not begin with much programming at the new sites. Pastor Larry Osborne explained the result. "It was hard for them to bring in new people and assimilate new people when part of their identity was back on, if you will, the main campus. The children's and youth programs would always be automatically second class if it's not self-contained. . . . When we were just telling them, 'Oh you come and join main campus midweek or whatever.' They were very much kind of the weaker sister."

Osborne explains their new approach: "Going forward when we plan a campus, even if it's six to ten miles away, it needs to be as self-contained as possible. Its own youth program, its own children's program, everything. . . . In reality, niche ministries can be very powerful. For instance, right now we have one campus with a little more than four hundred in attendance, and they had fifty high schoolers last weekend. That's a phenomenal percentage that we could never get with our big huge ministry."

Windermere Ministries has come to the opposite conclusion. Chuck Carter feels, "It's a constant reminder. Every week they come to the main campus that is part of something bigger. They are reminded of why we are doing it, why we are part of something bigger—we weren't satisfied to be a holy huddle of a campus that was full. We had a mission to accomplish."

Clearly knowing who you are and what matters will guide you in making these defining decisions.

Priority One:
Finding the Leader

For the last four years, I have spent a weekend each February as a counselor on a preteen retreat that my church conducts for fourth to sixth graders. The preteens have a choice of activities on Saturday, and I volunteer to help with a challenge course. This includes several challenges that the ten to fifteen preteens who elect the activity need to do together.

Each challenge teaches principles of working together, listening to each other, and valuing the unique contribution of each preteen. One of the activities consists of a large flat board (6 feet by 8 feet) resting on a log. The goal is for the whole group to sit or stand on the board while balancing it on the log for thirty seconds without the board touching the ground.

The first few minutes consist of each preteen moving on the board in the direction that they think will help. Invariably the weight shifts too far as more than one person shifts at one time. A good idea with good movement can tip the board too far if more than one preteen moves.

The group of preteens will never balance the board until there is a single leader who the others are willing to listen to and follow. One year the group never did balance the board even after trying a couple different leaders and spending fifteen minutes trying. Preteens kept shifting their weight without direction from their leader.

Leadership Is Needed

Effective leadership is not easy at a single-site church. As you move to multi-site, you are spreading people out across a bigger board that will be harder to balance. You are increasing the complexity of providing leadership exponentially. Without effective leadership and communication, the new site will flounder, tipping back and forth like the preteens who are moving without coordination.

Judges summarizes the days when "there was no king in Israel; everyone did whatever he wanted" (Judg. 21:25). Similarly, we get the same picture of people casting off restraint and doing their own thing in the proverb, "Without revelation people run wild" (Prov. 29:18). When leadership is not present, good ideas and good activities can prove to be unproductive or even counterproductive.

Leadership Must Flow

The temporary leadership provided by Israel's judges provides glimpses of greatness and potential for the people of God, but each instance was fleeting. This is a sharp contrast to the consistent flow of leadership shown in Exodus. God had clearly shown His leadership of the people out of Egypt and had shown the flow of that leadership in Moses. With the advice of his father-in-law, Moses continued the flow of leadership four more levels by appointing leaders "of thousands, hundreds, fifties, and tens" (Exod. 18:25).

As the theocracy continued after Moses' death, God reaffirmed the flow of leadership to Joshua. He not only named him the new leader, He used a miraculous crossing of the Jordan River to demonstrate that Joshua was the extension of His leadership over Israel.

Before this miraculous crossing, God said to Joshua, "Today I will begin to exalt you in the sight of all Israel" (Josh. 3:7). It should be our prayer that God would establish each senior pastor in the hearts of his people and that the flow of God's leadership continues from there.

Church polity varied significantly among the multi-site churches we studied. These included: pastor-led, pastoral team-led, staff-led, elder-led, pastor-led elder-protected, congregational, and board of directors. The larger size of these multi-site churches has led to more centralized models of leadership in these churches. While some maintain a congregational element to their polity, they have built processes to keep this from slowing progress until the next business meeting.

Regardless of a church's exact polity, it must intentionally establish a clear flow of leadership. Every extension of the flow is important. However, the roles vary at each extension of the flow.

The senior pastor or leadership team is responsible for establishing the church's identity (both beliefs and vision), values, and expression.

The campus pastor is responsible for communicating this direction and extending this direction to the site based on the context of their community.

The ministers responsible for ministries across campuses (e.g., student minister, worship minister, children's minister, etc.) also are responsible for establishing the direction for their ministry that fits within and supports the church's direction, identity, and values.

The core leaders at the new site are responsible for communicating and extending this church, campus, and ministry direction with their ministry team.

As you move through the flow, the leaders have less responsibility for establishing direction and more responsibility for contextualizing and implementing the direction.

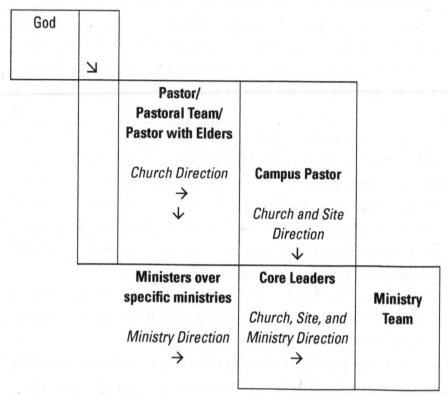

Figure 4: Leadership Flow

Joe Stowell, teaching pastor at Harvest Bible Chapel in Illinois, cuts to the heart of the matter: "For us so far, the Lord has really provided us A-plus people. But if you don't get the right guy as your campus pastor, you can just forget it."

The reason the campus pastor is mission-critical is "they are basically like a store manager," Stowell said. "They have to know how everything works."

Mark Batterson, pastor of National Community Church, affirmed their importance. "I think the key to multi-site is that you have got to have great campus pastors, people that are gifted and loyal and yet don't have to be in that lead pastor capacity."

Dan Scates, multi-site minister at LifeBridge Christian Church, summarizes, "Finding them and getting them raised up and trained is the biggest task that we have in front of us! And it's a tough one."

> *If you don't get the right guy as your campus pastor, you can just forget it.*

What Is a Campus Pastor?

One of the earliest ideas to emerge from first-generation multi-site churches was the concept of the campus pastor. Each site needed a "face with the place," a person to be the on-site leader for those in the church and the visible host for those visiting the church.

Every campus pastor we talked to could rattle off a multitude of things they do. In fact, the phrase, "You must be present to win," seemed to fit how they acquired many of these tasks. As the "face" who was always present, they "won" a lot of responsibilities.

If their role is not more defined than a list of tasks, then they will become overrun with even more tasks without really having direction or priorities.

Owen Nease is the campus pastor for the Stillwater campus of Henderson Hills Baptist Church. Henderson Hills had a job description for Nease when he arrived, but multi-site is new to all of them and Nease is the first campus pastor the church has had.

Nease describes, "It feels like there are several roles mixed together. What comes out of the oven is something called a campus pastor. There are elements of it that feel like an associate pastor. There are a lot of elements of it that feel like an education minister. There are times that I feel like the executive pastor. And then at the same time you are trying to get all these ministries started and rolling in a particular direction." He admits, "It's been tough to prioritize and figure out where do I spend my time."

Henderson Hills is not alone. Many new multi-site churches have left much of the campus pastor's role undefined as they learn the ropes. As long as the campus pastor takes the ball and moves it forward, it is looked on favorably. Little thought is given to clearly articulating the work of the campus pastor to truly maximize this position and the others around them.

Fortunately roles are beginning to solidify at some churches and others have learned valuable lessons related to campus pastors.

What Is the Campus Pastor's Role?

We need to know the tangible work we expect campus pastors to do. More importantly we need to understand how these tasks fit together to shape distinct roles they play in the church overall and on that campus.

Scott Chapman, copastor of The Chapel, pointed out, "When you look at a small church pastor, they are a jack-of-all-trades. And they have to be good enough in the pulpit, good enough at shepherding, and good enough at leadership to get the whole pie cut. Honestly, when they become very good at it, their church grows and they find themselves often in a crisis. And we looked at that and said it is amazingly hard because most people don't even get to that point. They get to a point and find, 'I can do one and a half of these and maybe two of these and not three.'"

Pastor Drew Hayes of The People's Church in Shelbyville, Tennessee, said, "The reason there are very few churches making an impact for Christ of any significance in rural and small and medium-size towns everywhere across America is because they don't have the pastoral leadership and communications ability." Hayes felt a personal calling to do something about it.

"I have always felt that if you could take a person who has a high leadership gift as well as a high ability in communication, plus a high-risk tolerance level, you could take that person and then multiply them into churches where the rest of the paid staff were more pastoral type people. Then you could really make much more of a difference.

"Most churches are not making much of an impact because their pastors aren't lined up to make an impact. And that's not their fault. They are great assistant pastors. They are great pastor-care people. But they are not great communicators and great leaders."

David McDaniel, Director of North Point Ministries at North Point Community Church, affirmed this perspective. "We've proven to ourselves . . . not to the world, but at least to ourselves that you can separate leader from communicator. . . . When you separate those roles, then you can say, 'Wow, I can get a really great leader that's not necessarily a great communicator or preacher.'"

Any pastor has three primary roles: teacher, shepherd, and leader. Most pastors tend to excel at one or two and they get by with the other—or worse, it may be a liability. The role of campus pastor is, in fact, an opportunity to avoid such liabilities. By the time you look at the role of the campus pastor, you should have maximized your church's plan for teaching and know who will do the teaching and how will they do it at your church (see chap. 4). It is important to point out that most multi-site churches choose to have a campus pastor even when they have multiple teachers. They realized, whether consciously or subconsciously, the value of having a campus pastor focus on shepherding and leading.

A campus pastor's roles are leadership and shepherding.

Chapman indicated that the balance between these two roles depends on the size of the site or the size you are planning for the site to become. The larger the site, the more the balance of the role shifts toward more leadership with a greater portion of the shepherding being decentralized. The smaller the site, the more the balance of the role shifts toward shepherding and caring for this fellowship with a smaller organization to lead.

Leadership

The campus pastor's leadership role means they are extending the senior leadership of the church to that site. This requires the campus pastor to understand and sincerely believe in the church's beliefs, vision, values, and expression. It is their role to embody this identity and direction and to communicate it.

Guy Melton, pastor of Oasis Church in South Florida, admits they made a huge mistake in their initial hiring of campus pastors. It actually took four tries to find a good fit. Melton was quick to point out that "we have a great relationship with all three men. They are all godly men." Yet the mistake Oasis made was "bringing in people at the beginning at the new campus that did not understand our vision, our philosophy, and the direction of where we are going.

"We will never do that again, even if it means we don't start another campus or we wait a year before we start a campus." To ensure that this happens, Melton states, "Our commitment as a pastoral staff is that the next person that does campus pastor for us on any campus has to spend six months to a year on our staff at Pembroke Pines." Oasis began this process with the third candidate, who realized after three months that it was not what he wanted.

Don Ruppenthal, associate pastor at RiverTree Christian Church, concluded, "It is real important from day one that your [campus] pastor knows what your DNA is and is stating that over and over from the beginning: 'Here is what we are about. Here is where we are heading. Here is where we are going.'"

Casting the vision is more complicated than it sounds. Robbie Stewart, West Lafayette campus pastor for Northview Christian Life Church, shared, "Most of the visioning for the congregation in general and where we are going happens within the context of the sermon. It makes it a little more difficult because the DNA, the vision of the main campus, is pretty well solidified, and then up here people are still learning it. I find that one of the difficulties I have not being able to actually teach is that I have to really look overtime for opportunities to kind of infuse this vision of what the church is."

This often occurs through a lot of personal meetings. Stewart observed, "Whenever someone wants to step up and do something,

I take the opportunity to try to make them understand why this specific ministry exists, how it fits into what we're doing."

The campus pastor is responsible for everything that occurs. He must be leading the leaders of each aspect of the site's organization as well as overseeing the facility itself. This can include transitioning from one rented facility to another. "You're a general manager," McDaniel summarized. "You're basically a senior pastor with all the responsibilities, except you're not preaching."

To emphasize the need for firm leadership, consider the fact that some members within your church may see the new site as an opportunity to promote some things that wouldn't fly at the original campus. In addition, you may attract members of nearby churches hoping your new site will become what they can't get their church to become.

Ruppenthal noted, "It's not like the people aren't godly people: they just have a different agenda." If any of these ideas, programs, or directions are not the identity, values, and approach of your church, they must be rejected. The campus pastor must be equipped to identify such differences and keep the site moving in the same direction as the church.

Another aspect of the leadership role is representing the church in the community. Scott Chapman pointed out that a senior pastor has "a certain relational capacity" to spend time on relationships with the other churches in the area. The campus pastors of a church allow this capacity to grow. "We make one of the metrics of performance for every one of our campus pastors that they establish ten significant friendships with pastors in their community." This external investment in other churches has expanded the ministry impact of The Chapel exponentially.

Shepherding

Mike Brisson, associate pastor at Cornerstone Community Church, oversees the multi-site ministry and works alongside the campus pastor at their Temecula campus. "Myself and the campus pastor, we really have to be cheerleaders and really affirm and keep the enthusiasm high."

Ruppenthal indicated the type of men who have worked well as campus pastors. "The guys we have, they love people, they love pastoring to people."

One church that has not had campus pastors per se, has had to change how they utilize their teaching pastors because they have seen a void in the area of shepherding. Brodie Taphorn, community leader at Upper Arlington Lutheran Church, indicated that their senior pastor learned this firsthand from members in a series of focus groups. "One of the things he heard our church saying to the leadership was, not so much we want to know our pastor, but we want our pastor to know us."

Assigning this shepherding responsibility to the campus pastor is a critical part of their role and one that attendees need.

Barry Galloway echoed the mentoring aspect of the campus pastor role. "Up here in the mountains, many people had not been pastored and really hadn't developed and grown up under leaders. So I really get to spend a lot of time growing, not only reaching out, but growing people and growing these leaders deeper so they can reach out more themselves."

This leadership development role for Galloway also includes teaching leadership classes and identifying leaders.

What Kind of Person Makes an Effective Campus Pastor?

Multi-site leaders shared many helpful characteristics to look for in a campus pastor:

- "You must believe in what that senior pastor at the main campus is doing. You have to buy into the vision." —Barry Galloway, the Tehachapi campus pastor for Desert Vineyard
- "You have got to check your ego at the door because I may say something tomorrow that ticks somebody off. Well, it's real easy for them to go up the road and go to the other campus and still be connected. . . . They are still a part of the kingdom

work that we are doing here, and so it really forces you to have a kingdom mind-set." —Chuck Carter, pastor, First Baptist Church Windermere

- "Our mind-set is wanting to partner with people who have a call to ministry, who want to associate with something larger than just their own independent little church out somewhere." —Craig Gorc, senior associate pastor, Cedar Park Assembly of God

- "A person who demonstrates an actual call to ministry that is voiced by the way they talk about what they feel that God's put in their heart to do in the sense of building a church and a community. Second to that is the ability as a leader . . . that they demonstrate humility and have the ability to actually draw people to themselves and head them in a direction." —Craig Gorc, senior associate pastor, Cedar Park Assembly of God

- "They've got to be very, very strong in team building and team leading, and have a real evangelistic and external type of heart and focus. . . . [They must be] truly leaders that can motivate the people who are out there to reach these new communities and to shape the kind of place that we need." —Dan Scates, multi-site minister at LifeBridge Christian Church

- "You need to be able to lobby for the resources you need to make it happen. They don't necessarily have the seniority to come in and make people do stuff for them. They really need to be persuasive." —David McDaniel, director of North Point Ministries

- "They quite often end up being salesmen within the organization, trying to get people to do the things they need to get done." —David McDaniel, director of North Point Ministries

- It helps when people tend to want to help them because they are "naturally affable. But at the same time they can get stuff done." —David McDaniel, director of North Point Ministries

First, notice that these characteristics revolve around people. Second, they involve movement: drawing people in and sending them out. Drawing people in together is the shepherding role and sending them out productively within the vision of the church is the leadership role of the campus pastor.

Seacoast Church is a first-generation multi-site church that has invested in many other multi-site churches by sharing things they have learned. Frequently the multi-site churches we interviewed cited Seacoast as a church they studied prior to becoming multi-site. Geoff Surratt, pastor of ministries at Seacoast Church, has the following advice based on his experience determining the qualities of a successful campus pastor.

Geoff Surratt

pastor of ministries, Seacoast Church

From 1988 through 2001 Seacoast Church grew from zero to a little more than three thousand weekend attenders; from 2002 through 2008 we grew from three thousand to almost ten thousand weekend attenders, an increase of more than 300 percent. Two factors fueled this incredible growth: our decision to become one church in multiple locations and the emergence of the role of campus pastor. Each of our thirteen campus pastors is unique; they include a farmer, a dentist, and an electrician, but their collective impact on Seacoast has been nothing short of spectacular. Nothing impacts the growth and success of a campus more than the leadership of an effective campus pastor.

What does an effective campus pastor look like? This has been a tough question to answer. They have a lot in common with a senior pastor, but they are not the primary leader and often they do not

---

speak on the weekends. They are similar to other staff pastors, but they often lead large congregations with multiple ministries under them. There are really no models within a traditional church staff for the role of campus pastor.

I think the best example of what an effective campus pastor should look like is an NFL quarterback. Not that every campus pastor should be 6'5", 230 pounds, with a laser-rocket arm, although it probably wouldn't hurt. Actually the qualities that make a quarterback successful in the NFL are the same qualities that make a successful campus pastor.

Quarterback Qualities of a Successful Campus Pastor

1. A successful quarterback leads himself first.

To be successful in the NFL a quarterback has to have tremendous self-discipline. He has to memorize a massive playbook, he has to keep himself in peak physical condition, and he has to minimize distractions that can detract from his focus on the game. He has to continually sharpen his skills. It is not enough for a quarterback to be fast, strong, and smart; he must continually strive to be faster, stronger, and smarter than his opponent. Before a quarterback can lead his team, he must lead himself.

In the same way, a good campus pastor is successful at leading himself. He is self-disciplined, punctual, and organized (or he is able to delegate organization to others). He is a self-feeding learner who is continuously growing in his personal spiritual walk and in his understanding of ministry. A campus pastor who needs supervision and prompting or who lacks initiative will struggle.

2. A successful quarterback leads through his team.

Imagine Peyton Manning, quarterback of the Indianapolis Colts, deciding that if he wants something done he will have to do it himself.

He hikes the ball to himself, drops back into the pocket, spots himself open on the sideline, fires a bullet to himself, throws his own block, and sprints 40 yards for a self-made touchdown. Since he can't hold the ball and kick the extra point, he opts for a quarterback keeper up the middle. The reality is that Manning is only as good as his ability to lead through the team that is around him. While his personal skills are important, they are secondary to his ability to inspire, lead, and utilize a team.

I have seen churches look for campus pastors who are good public speakers, efficient administrators, or compassionate counselors. All of these are great qualities, but a great campus pastor has to be a great team builder and leader. He can learn to speak, he can hire an administrator, and he can train counselors, but there is no substitute for the ability to carry out a ministry plan through teams of inspired volunteers. To find a good campus pastor, look for an effective team and hire their leader.

3. A successful quarterback works within the coach's vision.

One of the most important things for a quarterback to understand is that he is not the ultimate leader of the team; the coach is the ultimate leader. The quarterback brings tremendous skills and the team would be crippled without him, but the coach casts the vision and sets the agenda for the team. The coach decides if they will be primarily a passing team or if they will rely mostly on the running game. The coach determines if they go for a first down on fourth and three or if they punt. A quarterback who cannot work with the coach's vision causes division on the team and prevents the team from achieving success.

A campus pastor has a similar role. While he is responsible for his own campus and he often leads a large team of his own, he is not the primary vision caster for the church. His job is to work within the framework and philosophy of ministry of his senior pastor. This can be a major challenge, especially when that philosophy changes.

A couple of years ago our senior pastor felt God leading him to make a major change in how we do our weekend services at Seacoast. He announced that we were going to begin serving communion every service even though our pattern had always been once a month. Although we didn't have a single cross in any of our auditoriums, he said that we were going to begin inviting people to pin their prayer requests to crosses every weekend. He even said we were going to add votive candles to our worship experience at each campus. Our campus pastors are not "yes men," so they had a lot of questions when Greg shared this new vision. But once they knew that Greg sincerely felt he had heard from God, they each were completely on board. They know that Greg is God's chosen leader for Seacoast, and they each operate within the vision God has given him for our church.

4. A successful quarterback improvises when necessary.

The difference between a good quarterback and a great quarterback is his ability to improvise. No matter how clever the offense, how carefully crafted the game plan or how precise the execution, there comes a time in every game when the quarterback has to call an audible. He can't check with the coach, discuss it with the team, or refer to the playbook. He simply relies on instinct and does what he believes to be best for the team at that moment. The great quarterbacks, the ones who win Super Bowls and make millions in endorsements, are masters of improvisation.

The ability to improvise is also key to a successful campus pastor. At Seacoast we have detailed guidelines for every ministry; we mentor, train, and monitor our campus pastors. But at the end of the day it is the ability of the campus pastor to respond to the unique needs of his congregation, which determines the success of his campus.

There is a well-known saying in the military, "No battle plan survives contact with the enemy." The same is true in multi-site ministry. There is no one-size-fits-all plan of ministry that applies in all situations and communities. An effective campus pastor understands the ministry plan and DNA of his church, but he also has the freedom and initiative to change and adapt ministry to meet needs.

Can you teach someone to be a great campus pastor?

What we have discovered at Seacoast is that you can teach the skills of being a campus pastor: how to conduct an effective weekend service, how to counsel, how to organize a staff. But the basic building blocks have to be in place first. When we are looking for a campus pastor, we look for someone who is already great at leading himself, leading through a team, working within a vision, and being able to improvise. When we find a leader like that, we know we have a potential Super Bowl winner on our hands.

Where Do You Find a Campus Pastor?

So where do you find someone who leads himself, who leads through his team, who works within the coach's vision, and who improvises when necessary? Where do you find someone who is friendly, outgoing, persuasive, magnetic, and motivational, yet is humble enough to follow the existing leadership and has taken the time to understand this vision?

Identifying the presence of these characteristics in someone rarely occurs in a single interview. It is something that is observed over time and emerges through ongoing dialogue. For many multi-site churches, this has led them to hire campus pastors from within.

Craig Gorc, senior associate at Cedar Park Assembly of God, explained, "We like to raise people up within our own system. And in the process of that, you get to know them and then their life is under your scrutiny."

Jeff and Eric were two active members of Cedar Park. Jeff led the divorce care ministry and Eric led the men's ministry. Gorc described them as "family guys" and "career guys." One is a pharmaceutical rep and one is a concrete salesman. Both had already proven their leadership skills and their ability to draw people to themselves. In addition, they had demonstrated a calling to pastoral ministry and were in preparation for credentialing for ordination.

One day Gorc sat down and threw out an idea: "What if you guys copastored this opportunity out here in a place called Duvall?" Gorc would never have posed this idea without first seeing their leadership skills in action, having invested in their pastoral training, and seen that they could work together. This site grew from about twelve people to seventy-five or eighty in its first year.

Healing Place rarely hires staff from outside the church. Marc Cleary and Dan Ohlerking shared, "We don't do résumés. We don't send out job applications for people that are graduating college. . . . That's just not how we do it."

The practice of hiring from within shifts the focus of hiring from an information-gathering blitz about a candidate to a long-term investment in training. Cleary and Ohlerking outlined the progression: "People come to the church, become a part of the church, and so by the time you've got somebody who is twenty-five years old and they want to be a campus pastor, they have gone through a lot of leadership. They know the DNA; they know the heart. . . . They are making it happen already. . . . So our campus pastors, we know all of them. We have known them for years and years. And so what we're doing is trying to just help equip them with the skills that they need for a campus pastor. . . . You don't have to face the challenge of people who may not have the same heart."

Harvest Bible Chapel has hired campus pastors both from inside and outside the church. Those hired internally had already been on staff for a while and knew how the church did things. Those they brought in from the outside required several weeks of intensive training. They spent time with every ministry team to learn how that ministry functions, what the success factors are for each area, and how to leverage the strengths of each one. This is critical as they oversee the interaction of each of these ministries on the new campus.

Several churches hired from outside the church, but actually hired people with ties to their church. RiverTree Christian Church hired someone that several staff members knew well as their first "lead pastor"—a campus pastor. The rough road that he faced had less to do with the fact that he was hired from the outside than that he was still getting acclimated to the church when the site launched.

As a result, he did not know people well enough to choose the core leaders. He did not know people in the community and initially did not live there, so it was difficult for him to help the church get established in the community.

This example illustrates an important principle about hiring a campus pastor: How long they have been a part of your church's ministry is more important than whether they are an internal or external hire.

What Characteristics of the Campus Pastor Vary by Strategy?

The strategic decisions you make related to who your church is and how your church will do multi-site impact the role and type of campus pastor you are looking for.

Choosing to utilize video teaching often means a campus pastor won't teach. Churches that do not have their campus pastors teach, must find someone with a pastor's heart who is willing not to preach each week. Barry Galloway shared, "My wife was really concerned because I've been a senior pastor for seven years and now I'm like a wheel under one, but I am OK with it because I believe in what we are doing here at this church."

A site that uses teaching via video has the personality and charisma of the teaching pastor on video each week. Barry Smith, pastor of Impact Community Church, pointed out that this must be reflected in the visible, campus pastor. "There needs to be some sort of a transition of that type of energy and the kinds of thing we have [on video] into a person that's visible right there in front of them that they can connect with."

The campus pastor should be a very visible and key part of the worship service because it allows him to communicate his care for the congregation as their shepherd. This time also allows him to keep the church's vision in people's minds and to motivate the congregation to be a part of that effort as their leader.

Churches that intentionally give their sites a large degree of autonomy look for different things than those who desire to replicate a very similar experience. Christ the King Community Church encourages a more free organic growth. Dave Browning explained, "Our story is ideally suited for a pastor-preneur, somebody willing to take risks, wants to start new things, wants to go new places, wants to reach out to adjacent communities, wants to even have a ministry in other states or countries. If somebody wants to do that sort of stuff, then we're saying, 'Sic 'em!'"

In contrast, LifeBridge is trying to create sites very much like the original church. "For us, we are trying to duplicate a lot of the good things about LifeBridge at a site," Scates summarized. Since LifeBridge has an identity, values, and an expression for their church, "what we're asking someone to do is carry that out in their context."

Why Do You Need to Find the Campus Pastor First?

Finding a campus pastor is the first order of business sequentially now that you have begun to plan for your new site. The campus pastor embodies your church's pastoral leadership at that site. Once you are sure you have found an individual who is on the same page in terms of vision and direction for your church and how your church will function across multiple sites, you need to begin to invest in this person.

Reinforce their commitment to this direction by immersing them in it if they have not already served on your staff. Then begin to empower them by involving them in the next steps of choosing a location and recruiting core leaders.

The more time that a new campus pastor can grow with these plans and the longer the campus pastor owns this responsibility, the greater clarity they will have in the leadership they provide to others. These early days allow senior leaders to invest in the campus pastor before they are spending significant time at the new site itself. It also allows the campus pastor to get to know the new site's community.

Dan Scates likens the process to planting a church. "We want to have someone in the community that's living there six months prior to launch. We want that person, the lead guy, meeting people, building community relationships, helping to tap into people that we have from [the original campus] that live out there and begin to organize them."

Some of the strongest appeals for lining up a campus pastor first came from campus pastors we interviewed.

Owen Nease admitted, "It has worked out great, but we almost tried to move too quickly into it. You need to have your campus pastor on board for a significant amount of time before you make the jump to the new campus."

Nease recommends nine months to a year of lead time with the campus pastor. He only had three months before they launched. He explained why a longer time on staff before the launch is needed: "You can read all the books you want, but like most jobs, until you find yourself in the middle of it . . . it is truly an on-the-job learning experience. So that's why I would say, 'Get that person on board.' Give them a chance to go around, talk with other churches who are doing this, and get a feel for what they are doing."

Don Ruppenthal recounted some of these same key principles as he shared how they would do their first site differently, knowing what they know now. RiverTree Christian Church hired the campus pastor in July for an October launch. If RiverTree could do this again, "we would have them on board early, but we would have them choose their team, be part of that whole process. And we would also have them be present in the area" of the new site. "You really have to have their presence in the community. That is so important."

For the campus pastor to be part of choosing a core team of leaders for the new campus, they have to be present at the church long enough to get to know potential leaders. As the plan begins to take shape, the first priority of finding a campus pastor naturally flows into the second priority of finding the core leaders.

CHAPTER
SIX

Developing a Team
of Leaders

ational Community Church in Washington, D.C., had five hundred people attending their church when they launched a second site. "I think that should be an encouragement to younger churches and smaller churches," Pastor Mark Batterson pointed out. "You don't have to be a church of ten thousand people to go multi-site."

So how did a church of five hundred find enough willing leaders to start down this path? It started with who they are as a church. Batterson described the people of National Community Church, saying, "They have the 'empty seat' DNA, which is huge!" This outward focus of always looking to bring a friend and welcome a visitor created a willing audience when the question of "who will help launch the next campus?" was asked.

Batterson noted, "We survey everything; we are always trying to get feedback from our congregation." So when they began to think about launching a new site, it was natural to survey the congregation about it. They asked about potential locations and other launch factors. But the key question was, "Would you be interested in being a part of a launch team?" Batterson recalled, "That question was a key barometer for us. Our goal internally was one hundred people. We felt like if we had one hundred people, we could successfully launch something.

"We took the survey and ninety-nine people said that they definitely or probably would be a part of that launch team." Batterson remarked, "I hadn't filled out a survey. So, in a sense, we had one hundred on the dot! That was a tremendous kind of affirmation and confirmation from the Lord that this vision was from God. The survey certainly confirmed that it was God's timing to step out in faith and launch another location."

Developing a Core Team of Leaders

Marc Cleary and Dan Ohlerking of Healing Place Church indicated that first they put a campus pastor in place who is called and equipped to be campus pastor. Then they ask, "Do we have the support staff of volunteers underneath those campus pastors to really meet the needs of the people?"

As your church examines who you are and what matters, you determine which ministries are a necessary part of your church's beliefs, vision, values, and expression. These core ministries are the ones you will prepare for the launch of your new site. You will need to choose a leader for each core ministry at the new site.

Figure 4: The Core Team of Leaders

What Matters? The core ministries you will have at launch	→	Core Leaders A leader for each core ministry

It is easy to try to skip this step and jump further down the flow of leadership as you recruit. However, these core leaders are a critical link in the leadership flow. When an angry parent wants to know who is in charge of their children, they will want to talk to the one leader of your children's ministry on that campus. When the worship team has a special request for the set-up team the following week, they will want a single person to contact. When the campus pastor is trying to invest in his leaders, he cannot do this for all the volunteers effectively. He must focus on the core leaders. These are his "span of care." They in turn invest in the volunteers on their ministry team.

Crossroads Community Church refers to their core leaders as "champions." Each of the champions takes responsibility for one of the ministries at the new site. For Crossroads, these include Kids Link, student ministries, worship, small groups, set up and tear down, prayer team, and First Impressions team. All of these champions are leaders who make up the leadership team at that campus.

Owen Nease of Henderson Hills Baptist Church described the same one-two punch. "Bring the campus pastor on board early on. I think there is an equal importance to identifying that worship leader and children's ministry coordinator. Whatever would be your major programs and coordinator for that program to identify that person early on as well because they need to buy in alongside the campus pastor with what is going on. And they need to understand their role." Without this early start, Nease warned, it really slows things down.

Churches that are planning a large site launch may be hiring part-time or even full-time core leaders. However, this is the exception rather than the rule. Examples of initial staffing are provided in chapter 9. Most new site launches have a core team that is primarily volunteers.

The core leaders at LifeBridge Christian Church's sites are volunteers with the exception of a part-time children's coordinator. Their campus pastor helps find core leaders for ministries such as worship, children's ministry, and student ministry. Then each minister on staff supports and resources their leader at that site. Multi-site minister Dan Scates summarized, "We need to find these key people and help them build the teams that are needed before we launch."

Marines or Missionaries?

Every church has Christian marines. You know who they are. They are the people who jump to volunteer when a new ministry emerges. Just like the slogan of the U.S. Marines Corps, "First to Fight," Christian marines want to be the first to see action. They are motivated and dedicated to the new task. They don't understand why everyone else is not on board.

Multi-site is not a ministry. It is who your church is or is about to become. Your church will need some marines to help you have a successful launch. They will give 110 percent to help make this work.

I first heard this concept from two of Community Christian Church's campus pastors as they described their experience. When they held an informational meeting about starting a new site, there were many people in attendance with varying degrees of interest. Following the meeting, some people quickly signed up and said, "Count me in."

At first, the campus pastor thought that this was his core group. Then weeks later some of those who asked the toughest questions at the meeting, who he thought might even be against starting the new site, came to him one at a time. They not only were ready to join the team, they were ready to sell their homes and move into the community where the site was being launched.

Community Christian called this second group missionaries. They are not just rallying around a leader or following a command, they are surrendering to a call. These are the ones who are in it for the long haul.

In contrast, marines will be the first to move to the next new ministry. For that reason, you cannot launch a site with marines alone. You will need both marines and missionaries to have a successful launch, but the majority of your core leaders need to be in this for the long haul, dedicated to the long-term success of the new site.

Mike Miller, director of ministry support for Community Presbyterian Church, described the group who launched their

Tassajara extension. "We moved one hundred people out there two years ago who agreed to be out there for a year. And I would say half of them have come back." In those two years, CPC @ Tassajara added about one hundred new people and was running one hundred fifty in attendance at that time.

Some of those who returned to the original campus returned because more programs were offered there. For others, it was never their intent to stay at the Tassajara site, but they were willing to go and help start the church. For others, the hard work was too tiring or they were disenchanted by meeting in a school. Miller indicated the biggest incentive to return to the main campus was the fact that all of the midweek activities had to be done at their main campus, because they could not rent the school during the week.

In the same way people change classes, change small groups, and change which service they attend, they also will change campuses. How you recruit core leaders and their teams can help minimize this. Seek people who are at the site to do more than fulfill a commitment. You want to avoid an undertow of people leaving that slows the waves of progress you are making. The growth rate of this new site determines how disruptive such departures will be.

Look among Your Best Leaders in Your Target Community

Mark Batterson pointed out that they have become proficient at setting up shop in new locations. While the logistics have gotten easier, getting leadership in place has not. One way they ease the process at National Community Church is to tap experienced leaders.

"It's just a question of people recommitting to that new location, and figuring out where they fit in terms of ministry, and then filling the holes that they leave in the places that they leave, because most of them were ministry leaders who are actively involved in our other locations."

Larry Ali, executive pastor of Desert Vineyard Christian Fellowship in California, said, "We have taken people who have been some of our best who happen to be from that community, and they have formed the core."

While this advice will fit most efforts to launch new sites, it won't fit those churches starting sites in locations where they do not have a base of members. Where do core leaders come from in these instances?

Launching a site in a new community in which you do not have a base of members functions much more like a church plant. Often this is done by first starting a small group Bible study or two. As these begin to grow and new groups are started, the base of leaders begins to emerge.

One of the larger multi-site churches that has started several sites in new communities is LifeChurch.tv. A core group in a distant new community often includes people the church already knows. Bobby Gruenewald, pastor and innovation leader, explained that these include "people that either have flexible jobs that allow them to relocate or people who are willing to actually leave the jobs that they have and move to a new location knowing that we are going to be starting a campus there."

In addition, Gruenewald indicated, "There are people in each of the communities that already have a connection to our church, typically through the Web. It could be family members of people that live near one of our other campuses. It could be people that have moved" to that city previously.

These unknown or latent connections to a new community often surface potential leaders. Gruenewald summarized, "The combination of all of this is where we will pull together a core group of people that want to be a part of serving and volunteering and a part of really the ground floor work that's involved in getting something built."

Valley Bible Fellowship asked some of their California congregation and staff to go to Las Vegas to help launch that site. Senior pastor Ron Vietti observed, "We didn't keep many of them there. Most of them wanted to come back to Bakersfield in a time frame because they were used to a big church mentality . . . and also a cultural difference between

Bakersfield grassroots type of living and the Vegas big city. That was hard. Then we did ask some of the Vegas people that were talented to come to Bakersfield to help us and they didn't stay; they didn't like the transition. So really I think the key to the multi-site venues is to try to raise people up in that city to take on the ministry responsibilities."

Now that is a missional mind-set!

Rick Rusaw, author of *The Externally Focused Church*, also shares a missional mind-set and seeks to instill that in the leaders at LifeBridge Christian Church. Rusaw shares practical advice as he shares their story.

> *"I think the key to the multi-site venues is to try to raise people up in that city to take on the ministry responsibilities."*

Rick Rusaw

senior minister, LifeBridge Christian Church

When we launched our first multi-site (Tri-Towns Campus), it was about twelve miles from our current location. It was also an area that because of housing prices in surrounding communities was growing with young couples, starter families, and recently retired. This community also included a lot of people who already had a connection to LifeBridge. This was both a blessing and a curse: a blessing in that we had connections and relationships, and a curse in that many were content to do what they had been doing.

The thought of meeting in a school gym and watching a video message without many of the things they had grown accustomed to, was not their first choice. This is a great opportunity for me to say thanks to our Tri-Towns folks who were our guinea pigs in doing multi-sites.

Even now, after several years and three campuses, and with two more ready to launch, we consider ourselves neophytes at this whole multi-site venture. A couple of things were critical to our sites.

Begin with the End in Mind

At LifeBridge we want people to *discover grace, grow in grace,* and *live gracefully.* That expresses itself in finding ways to reach new people (not just look to swap sheep around), encouraging people to get in a small group or other growth opportunity, and to serve— whether they serve in or out of the church doesn't matter as long as they are serving others and honoring God.

When a launch date for Tri-Towns was set, we backed up from that date and did all the things that most site launches or church plants do. We also started finding out with whom we already had a connection. Those we knew weren't in a group we connected into some small groups. We encouraged them to host several events to which they could invite their friends. We immediately connected with the public schools, the city leaders, and asked what kind of ways we could serve them.

Before the site launched, opportunities emerged to build relationships within our church family who lived there, meet a lot of new people, and find ways to be of benefit to the community.

Part of the DNA of our church is to be externally focused. We wanted no less for our sites, and we have made it a priority to first find ways to serve in a place where we are going to launch a campus. The credibility and relationships that are established have been valuable to the success of our sites.

Just recently Steve McCarthy, our Johnstown campus pastor, was asked to cochair a countywide emergency management services commission. This happened because while the site is only two years old and has an attendance of two hundred, the site has been active in serving the community for nearly three years and has been involved in a number of ways assisting the community with needs. After tornadoes affected several surrounding communities with severe damage, it was volunteers from our Johnstown campus who were among the first to be contacted to help coordinate relief. Why? Because they had already established great relationships and demonstrated care for the community.

We will not launch a new campus without finding ways to already be serving in the community for six to twelve months ahead of the launch. We want our sites to be externally focused—and to see serving the community as a critical part of who we are. Serving has provided credibility, opened doors of opportunity, and created relationships that have been vital to the health and viability of each campus.

Volunteers Are the Lifeblood

If you do ministry in any way, shape, or form, we all recognize how important getting and keeping volunteers can be. Our first site launched with a campus pastor who also was responsible for small groups for the entire church and volunteers in key spots. Our second site launch began with a part-time campus pastor and part-time children's pastor. Everything else is led by volunteers. Multi-site increases dramatically the opportunities for people to be involved in ministry. Here is what we have seen happen in the two additional campuses we have launched.

1. People who had never volunteered for any ongoing involvement got engaged.

With both launches we found people who were part of our congregation yet had never really found a way to be substantially involved in serving. Interestingly enough, all of our current campus pastors were volunteers in the life of our church on our main campus. One of our members said it this way: "I used to come and be active in attending but always thought they had plenty of people to help; now I realize that there were always opportunities to get involved and I couldn't hide behind the 'someone else will do it' mentality." We had a substantial increase in new volunteers at both new campuses.

2. New leaders emerge.

Not one team leader had been a leader on our main campus. There were some who had been involved, but none had been leading. The new campuses provided the opportunity and necessity of raising up new leaders.

3. Involvement brought a deeper connection.

This isn't any kind of news flash. We all recognize that as people get engaged their commitment often deepens. Our sites have provided opportunity for broader involvement, deeper relationships, and stronger connections. Ownership and community are two immediate benefits that come from enlisting volunteers.

4. Closing the distance created more social connection.

People who were attending our main campus from another community often didn't or couldn't get their friends and neighbors to join them. When the church moved to their neighborhood, their natural connections and community involvement opened the doors to get their friends to join them. Each of our new campuses have found that more than 75 percent of the attendees had no previous connection to LifeBridge. Whether the distances we are closing are proximity, social, or cultural, closing those distances people have to "travel" is critical.

We decided at the beginning that we wanted to get people engaged and that we would have to discover ways to fill critical roles with volunteers. It isn't that we don't believe there is a need for paid staff, but rather that we believe that nurtured and supported through our paid staff, volunteers can have a tremendous impact in the life of our congregation. Building volunteer teams and leaders has become the primary job description of staff. Dan Scates, who coordinates our multi-site effort on our staff, says, "We only want half of the volunteer jobs filled at launch so we can invite new people into service." Service is the front door at LifeBridge.

Empower the Core Leaders

Once you have found the core leaders, their commitment must be cultivated.

Create a Sense of Ownership

Mike Brisson, associate pastor at Cornerstone Community Church in California, described one of the challenges they faced was "finding the right people with the right gifts and the right heart. It is not just a warm body. You need to find somebody that really has an entrepreneurial spirit about them. They like challenges, they like the task of new ministry opportunities, people that will feel a sense of ownership."

"When I have my leadership team meetings, I don't necessarily come with the answer," said Chuck Babler, campus pastor of the White Pines campus of Crossroads Community Church. "I try to get all of their input. . . . So giving people that ownership and buy-in is especially key because it is a lot of work."

You may find that there are some tasks that need to be rotated at the new site, but be careful as you consider this. It can be a sign that you have not created the necessary level of buy-in and can create some other negative consequences.

Barry Smith indicated that very few people enjoyed going to Impact's new site. "It became a necessary evil to fulfill and resource in the name of outreach and evangelism. So with that in mind then, the set-up and tear-down team was all on a rotation basis. The greeters and ushers were all on a rotation basis. The worship team was all rotation basis, which is probably the biggest problem we had."

The rotation in some areas may have been productive, but on their off week most volunteers returned to Impact's original campus. "When you've got all these people that are rotating in and putting in their time, the new people when they are coming are seeing all these different faces. There was no one really to connect with. 'This is my greeter. This is my usher. This is the person that serves me coffee and a Danish pastry.' It was all just random people putting in their time. So when you're just putting in your time, there is no ownership and no excitement and devotion to what's happening there."

Smith advised, "Anything involving the people—the worship team, the ushers and greeters, hospitality—get as many of those people [as possible] to say, 'This is my venue. This is my church. This is where I go.'"

Mike Brisson described a similar mistake Cornerstone Community Church made with their worship teams early in the life of their Temecula campus.

> We have a large church so we have multiple worship teams that are playing at all the different venues that we have. So we had one team to commit to going down there and launching [the Temecula site] and they played four weeks in a row, the first four weeks, then they were going to go to two weeks a month and then we were going to supplement that with two other teams to come in the other two weeks. Well, the problem that we discovered was that team really looked at it as a short-term commitment. Because some of the team members have teenagers involved up in the Baxter campus, it was inconvenient for their families to be going back and forth.
>
> At the end of summer, a worship leader that we were using one weekend a month stepped up and volunteered to be the main worship leader down there for a minimum of three weeks

out of every month. So now he is the worship leader at the Temecula venue and because of that he feels a stronger sense of ownership and really wants to contribute in more ways than just leading worship. He is even hosting barbecue and pool parties.

Invest in Your Core Leaders

Core leaders must understand and buy into the identity, values, and expression of the church. Then they must be entrusted with their respective ministry at the new site. They are accountable to the campus minister and to the minister over their ministry for all campuses, yet they are responsible for that ministry at that site.

Northland, A Church Distributed models this even at the recruiting stage, by not having the central staff recruit all the needed leaders. They start by recruiting only the core leaders. Tim Tracey, the executive director of worship, shared the progression: "They meet together for three months and then they begin building teams of volunteers and then they go through training." Although staff from the central campus helps with this training, they have already begun to empower the core leaders with the recruiting and elements of the training. In total, it is a three- to six-month process for Northland."

"If you haven't built a relationship," pointed out Michele Cox, "and gotten to know somebody and know their heart inside and out, and know that we are really in this thing together. We really have the same goal, the same passion, and the same heart. If you don't have that, what is going to happen when struggles come? People are going to walk away."

Cox is administrative assistant and one of only two staff hired to launch the White Pines campus of Crossroads Community Church. She recalls their original core group of twenty to thirty people met for six to eight months prior to launching their site.

"We met on a regular basis as a group," Cox described. "We did Bible studies, . . . we did a lot of praying, and then we worked through details time and time again. What that did was it not only helped us to figure out what we needed to do, but we developed relationships amongst each other so that we were committed not just to the vision of the church . . . but we were committed to each other."

Brisson shared, "We are regularly calling and e-mailing our team leaders and encouraging them to be in contact regularly with their volunteers. We do leadership barbecues where we get together and give them a 'that a boy!' We will even invite the senior pastor to come, and that is encouraging to them so they don't feel like they are separated."

One of the best forms of preparation is to have a chance to practice. One form of practice is to have several weeks of a soft-launch for the new campus at the new site. This means you do everything you plan to do on that campus, but you don't invite any new people. This allows you to make sure people are in place, the teams are working together, and the people know the equipment.

A second form of practice is to run parallel programs at your original campus for a period of time. Windermere Ministries did this as they prepared to launch a new campus. This was a significant launch in which the senior pastor and the longtime worship leader were moving to the new campus. Ultimately about 35 percent of the congregation moved with them to launch this new site.

Chuck Carter described this parallel time of preparation. "We took about six months before the grand opening and started sharing responsibilities at that point. Everything from [senior pastor] Mark Matheson and I switching back and forth preaching every other week to building two children's ministry teams and building two student teams." This did not mean things were stable on launch day. In fact, Carter described it as a "madhouse for a couple months." However, leaders had not just been identified on paper; they had literally been put in place ahead of time.

Create Critical Mass

Your core leaders are the ones who will lead the initial core ministries you will offer at the new site. However, they cannot do it alone. Furthermore, if you are effective at reaching your true target, the lost, it will take time before those you reach will be ready for many leadership positions.

Beyond the core leaders, others from your sending campus will move to the new campus. The fastest growing and healthiest new sites take to the new site a "critical mass" of laity who each have a responsibility at the new site.

Windermere Ministries took what they learned with their first site launch and applied it to their next launch. Carter explained, "We learned from the Lake Buena Vista model that if we were going to really get a critical mass out of [the original campus], we were going to really have to give them an incentive to do that." Having the senior pastor move to the new site was what they did to create this incentive that led a third of the congregation to make the move.

Critical mass can also be accomplished with site selection itself. When Harvest Bible Chapel launched their Elgin campus, they used a map to encourage people to shift to the new campus. "We kind of drew a line," Joe Stowell explained. "One Sunday we told people, 'If you live west of [highway] 59, you should go to the Elgin campus.' We didn't police it, but that is what we told people."

Whether or not you literally draw a line, creating critical mass must be a key consideration in selecting your location. This will be discussed in more detail in the next chapter.

Bottom Line: Leadership Comes First

I can't thank Barry Smith, pastor of Impact Community Church, enough for his transparency in discussing their first attempt at creating a second campus. Sometimes we learn best through disappointment.

An experience that doesn't work out as planned allows us to find some things that nobody would have considered essential until they are missing.

Smith realizes that at their new site, there wasn't strong leadership "that really caused people in their various aspects of that ministry—video, sound, lighting, singing, and musicians, all of that—to raise the bar and develop leaders within the ministry, to raise the bar so that there would be ownership and pride and excitement in that venue."

Impact was not able to truly establish a core leadership team. Without core leaders who were bought into the new campus, it became impossible to transfer a high commitment level to the other leaders who had responsibilities. "There was a lack of ownership from anyone that this is my venue. This is my church."

Smith takes responsibility for the shortcomings of this venture. Ultimately, each of the factors he described came down to a breakdown in the progression of leadership. Impact did not have a true campus pastor in place to extend Smith's leadership to this campus. They then had difficulty forming that group of core leaders. Finally, without effective core leaders they had little chance of mobilizing a critical mass of leaders willing to take on consistent responsibilities at the new campus and make it their church home.

Where Do You Launch?

I first met Jimmie Davidson during interviews with "Standout Churches" who had been evangelistically effective for ten straight years. His evangelistic passion had already led Highlands Fellowship to explode in tiny Abingdon, Virginia, and beyond. The tireless pursuit of sharing the gospel that Davidson, his staff, and congregation demonstrates will challenge your thinking regarding where to launch a site.

Jimmie Davidson

senior pastor, Highlands Fellowship

How to Decide Where to Launch a Site

For Highlands Fellowship multi-site is about more of us in more places for the global glory of God. *"We should make plans—counting on God to direct us"* (Prov. 16:9 LB). We do that because choosing can be messy.

I hope I can encourage you with what God is doing through the Highlanders and some of the ideas we are working on to be the missional people God has called all of us to be. I'll take you on a quick journey to show you how we decided where to launch. I can tell you up front, I'VE BEEN SCARED TO DEATH ON EVERY CHOICE! I was afraid of missing God. I was afraid of failure. I was afraid of sinking the whole ship.

What drives us is a Holy Discontent that causes us to move past our fears and take Christ to people not being touched with the good news. Over and over in Scripture He opens His broken heart and tells us how much it means to Him that the lost sheep are found, the lost coins are recovered, and the prodigals come home. I think our greatest barriers in deciding where to go are ourselves. We want the perfect places. There are none. Once when Jesus was asked to stay, He replied, "I must go into the other towns and preach the good news there also." He was on a mission. He hasn't changed; neither should we. *"There is no fear in love. But perfect love drives out fear, because fear has to do with punishment"* (1 John 4:18 NIV). Your first decision is to cast away that fear and follow Jesus. It's amazing how freeing that is! Once you've done that, it's now time to decide.

1. Take a baby step.

We simply took a wise risk and opened another site in another room inside of our existing building. We took a few steps outside of our main worship area to an underused room and created our first new site. All we needed was a little paint, a café atmosphere with Tennessee Volunteer Orange on the walls (OK, some Virginia Tech colors too), a few cool coffee choices with a projector, and we were up and running. People stood in line twenty minutes for the new site. The site was small with seating for seventy-plus people. Our little core group that signed up to get it started could not get in. I can still hear the crack of the bat as this idea went over the fence! In the weeks, months, and years since that first site, scores of people have found a place where they can feel comfortable and find Christ. We had our first win at Highlands Fellowship and realized it was time to take bigger risks and bigger steps. The truth is your first site may be right in front of you. Multi-site can begin anywhere.

2. Go with who you have and where they live.

Jesus is serious about this loving your neighbor thing and that includes sharing the good news. One of my favorite Bible verses is Acts 17:26–27. I love it because any time someone makes fun of my accent (grew up in a small town in Virginia in the Appalachian mountains), I can rebuke him or her for making fun of God! I love that verse! God places all of us in a place for a purpose! *"From one man he made every nation of men, that they should inhabit the whole earth; and he determined the times set for them and the exact places where they should live. God did this so that men would seek him and perhaps reach out for him and find him, though he is not far from each one of us"* (NIV). I love that! When I traveled to the Middle East, I was shocked to find God was already there. God is the master strategist. He wants to reach out through you to others.

Acts 17 for us meant a fifteen-minute drive on Interstate 81 and a city called Bristol, Virginia. Highlands Fellowship was growing in our small town, and people were beginning to drive longer and longer distances to get to us. In fact, one-third of our database was from Bristol. Our new site started with those we had and where they lived. I've noticed God gives every church what I call 82nd Airborne people ready to be the first in. They are pioneers. We had approximately 120 people commit to starting our new campus. We removed the barrier of distance and our fear of hurting our Abingdon campus and began Highlands Fellowship @ Bristol in January 2006. The Bristol campus has grown to more than eight hundred people in average attendance.

3. Listen for God's voice through others.

In deciding on our next site, we choose a bigger risk. Baby steps . . . baby steps. I've always said (thanks, rw), never let the fear of striking out keep you from taking a swing. For years we would have a few individuals visit Highlands and ask, "Will you ever come to Johnson City, Tennessee?" Johnson City is forty-five minutes away from our Abingdon campus. We would always boldly proclaim, "No." Dumb answer.

Like the apostle Paul when he heard the man from Macedonia, we began to sense God calling us through others to start a site in Johnson City, Tennessee. We wanted to see if God could use us to reach people in a city where we had almost no influence and almost no one attending from that area. It would be like starting a brand new church. Risky stuff! We visited some of the leading churches and concluded Highlands was different enough in style and approach to warrant our going in to reach those no one else would reach. We launched large with a direct mail, rented facilities on Sunday, and attracted more than three hundred people. Over a year later we are averaging two hundred twenty in attendance with a bivocational pastor who was a member at the Bristol Campus.

4. Leave no one out.

Let me give you one more story because God is so creative! He will often do things in the exact opposite way you thought of. We began thinking about Marion, Virginia. Marion does not mean much to most of you because it's a small declining town thirty minutes from the Abingdon campus with less than seven thousand people living there. Why would we go there?

I was called on a few years ago to do a funeral in a small Appalachian town an hour or so away from the Highlands campus in Abingdon. I will never forget as I followed the casket into the service with family members beside me weeping when one family member shared her thoughts. "Jimmie, my brother might have come to Christ had there been a Highlands Fellowship in this town." She was not accusing but just stating a fact. Jesus had changed her life at Highlands, and she longed for others to have the life she now had in Christ. I never forgot that. God planted that seed and it grew over the years. In fact it has become a fire burning inside me for small towns no one else is thinking about, for places others won't go.

As we thought about Marion we wondered, how do we reproduce ourselves in places with little income and declining populations? Last summer at a staff retreat it came to us, the little café idea. Remember our first site at Highlands? We took that idea, which has been so effective in reaching people, and reproduced it in a small town. A little band of people from Marion formed the core whose lives had been changed at Highlands. Highlands Fellowship @ Marion launched Easter of this year, 2008. Today we are averaging one hundred forty people in attendance.

There's no live music but a nursery, a preschool area, and a children's room upstairs with a café for adults on the main floor, all of this in 1,800 square feet. Since that launch in April a beachhead has been secured, and now we're preparing to add live music. The little café is one of the coolest places in town and people are buzzing about it to their neighbors. Lives are being changed.

In deciding where to go, we chose Jesus command, *"You will be my witnesses in Jerusalem, and in all Judea and Samaria, and to the ends of the earth"* (Acts 1:8 NIV).

We started where we were and with what we had, and we have no intentions of stopping there. We are on a journey to the whole world. Our goal is to launch nine more campuses by January 1, 2011. We will be launching sites while partnering with others around the globe that are doing so as well.

As I was finishing this article, we got word our little café idea has taken hold on the front lines of Afghanistan. The idea we shared and the supplies we sent are impacting our troops far away. E-mail was sent thanking us for the impact we are having on the troops, and a flag was flown on a combat mission next to the Pakistani border in honor of Highlands Fellowship. Jesus promised if you are faithful with what you have, no matter how small, He can trust you with more. That's our story. More of us going to more places, loving God and loving people because Jesus is already there. That's what God has revealed in Acts 17. He's already in the place you're thinking about. He just needs you to join Him.

An Expanded Vision

A key characteristic of multi-site churches and evangelistically effective churches is that they have a broader view of who God is calling them to reach than other churches. They reflect the "ands" in the work Jesus first gave His disciples: "You will be my witnesses in Jerusalem, *and* in all Judea *and* Samaria, *and* to the ends of the earth" (Acts 1:8 NIV).

A church's frame of reference must first move off of itself. When a church sees that its purpose is to reach those who do not know Jesus Christ, it will function differently. Your church cannot become an effective multi-site church if its frame of reference is inward. Your church cannot become an effective multi-site church if your vision for the future is limited to those you have reached in the past.

Listen to how these multi-site churches refer to the vision God has given their church. Notice that they are not referring to a small neighborhood, but a metro area or even a region of the country.

- "We believe that God has called us to the entire Temecula Valley." —Cornerstone Community Church
- "Our passion is for Long Island." —Shelter Rock Church
- "We felt a heavy burden for our region. And the way we define our region here is the South Florida, greater Palm Beach County area." —Christ Fellowship Church

- "We're going to be a multi-site church in the three counties of South Florida: Dade, Broward, and West Palm." —Oasis Church
- "We no longer think Columbia, Missouri, but within mid-Missouri and potentially around the world." —Woodcrest Chapel

As sites that would otherwise be separate churches work together in a multi-site, it fuels this expanded vision. For Chartwell Baptist Church, multi-site "enabled us to have a vision for reaching our communities in a way that wouldn't have been possible separately," explained Jim Carrie, executive and missions/outreach pastor. "I think it has given us the strength to really believe that we can significantly impact our communities for Christ."

Reach a City

The expanded vision for multi-site means even a different view of reaching one's city. Scott Chapman, copastor of The Chapel, shared that God is moving them to reach more of Chicago through additional sites, but their vision goes beyond that. "If we can create an entire network of churches that are passionate about seeing a spiritual awakening occur and you can spread that out, we feel you can see amazing things happen.

"No one church will ever reach Chicago. It is not possible. You need far bigger bandwidth. You need far more capabilities than that. It is not just a size issue. No matter how large or influential, it will never do that. But the church in Chicago can. And that is what gets truly exciting."

Craig Gorc, senior associate pastor at Cedar Park Church, admitted that their model "gives an impression maybe of a Catholic thing, and maybe that's more descriptive of what it is. Basically it is a centralized larger church in town with parish churches on the outer skirts of the town. . . . Our pastor uses the term, *Cathedral Church*.

"We are strategically looking for people who feel a call to pastor in an area that is on the edge of the population growth and on the edge of the geographic growth," Gorc continued. At the time of the interview,

Cedar Park had seven "branch" churches with attendance ranging from twenty-five to three hundred.

Other multi-site churches have added sites in their city that have allowed their church to cross physical boundaries that would have been difficult to cross without the new site.

For Spring Baptist Church located north of Houston, it meant crossing the freeway, with one site east and one site west of I-45. "We are reaching people over there at that campus that we would not have reached on the east campus simply because it is on that side of the freeway," said Pastor Mark Estep.

For Christ's Church in Jacksonville, it meant crossing a river and making the church accessible to more of the city in a reasonable drive time. "Jacksonville is the largest city in the country by land mass. And right through the middle of town is this river called the Saint John's River. And for some reason it's one of those big psychological things of crossing over the river. . . . So our big push and emphasis to reach out really was an outreach effort into this area," said lead pastor Jason Cullum.

Reach beyond a City or State

A local church can have locations that are not local. Yes, it is an oxymoron. Yes, it can be hard to envision. Yes, it can blur the lines between church and association of churches. But, yes, multi-site churches can have sites out of state, across the country, and even around the world.

The first example of a church with a vision that goes beyond their city will surprise many. It is not a megachurch in a large metro area seeking to crack America's top ten cities. The People's Church has sites in Shelbyville and Tullahoma, Tennessee. Their pastor, Drew Hayes, explained their vision. "We feel like our primary calling is in small and medium-sized towns—which is where we are."

The People's Church has an ambitious, God-sized vision, and multi-site is a key piece of it. "I want to take the model that will make an impact beyond just going back to baptizing people's kids and put it in communities that are small to medium sized where the people have never had access to the kind of church that is making a big imprint on their town and a difference in their communities."

In the last decade, several multi-site churches have launched out-of-state sites. Several of those churches we interviewed are among them including:

- Seacoast Church
- LifeChurch.tv
- Harvest Bible Chapel
- Christ the King Community Church
- Valley Bible Fellowship
- Heartland Community Church
- Crossroads Community Church

Bobby Gruenewald, pastor and innovation leader at LifeChurch, indicated that "there's certainly nothing magical about a state line that makes you more effective or less effective when you cross it."

Borders don't matter, but distance does. Distance limits the use of core leaders or critical mass from the existing site(s). Any site that is beyond a reasonable commuting distance will either resemble a church plant or require a merger with an existing church in that area. The typical multi-site church that has out-of-state locations utilizes video teaching across their sites.

In the case of Crossroads Community Church, their fourth site was unique. Not only was it started outside of Illinois where their first three campuses are located, it was started by the senior pastor. Keith Boyer and his wife along with a couple other families that were on staff relocated to the northeast side of Denver near Denver International Airport. This impact was felt at the new campus where 60 percent of the teaching would be recorded, but also at the original Freeport, Illinois, campus, which had been the "live" site since Crossroads became multi-site.

Reach beyond a Country

Christ the King and The Healing Place are two churches with locations in other countries. They did not start out pursuing overseas locations. Instead they were approached by believers in other countries who found their church by searching the Internet.

Dave Browning, senior pastor of Christ the King, shared one story: "All of our leaders in Africa are indigenous. A couple of key leaders in South Africa found us on the Internet and actually paid their way to come here to spend two weeks with us just to learn everything they could about what we are doing. One of them was an attorney who had a pretty successful law firm down there in Cape Town. He went back, took little video clips of our story on CD, and just went to all of his clients that he had had over the years. He walked into their offices, handed them the CD, and said, 'You know, this is something I want you to take a look at. And if you want to be a part of this, let me know.' He then walked out."

Browning continued, "And many of those business leaders and people have joined in the mission with us. They have said, 'This is what is needed.' And so it just spread leader to leader, town to town, country to country." In a matter of thirteen or fourteen months, there were eight worship centers each with more than one hundred people in Johannesburg alone.

One of the things that resonated with these leaders in Africa was the simplicity of Christ the King's organic, small-group-focused approach. "What we found," Browning explained, "is that the Western church model which was exported to Africa has been very burdensome on the continent. When we have gone over there and said, 'Well, yeah, you can have a church here. The first thing you need to do is build a building, and then the next thing you need to do is support a pastor full time.' Well, both of those things are just huge, huge mountains for those people to climb.

"So we have gone over there and said, 'Hey, you can start in your living room tonight if you want. Get some of your friends together.

Gather in Jesus' name and away you go.' And that is like a huge relief to the people over there."

Get to Know Your Target

God's evangelistic calling often comes in the form of a geographic area or a people group. By the time most missionaries join a mission, they feel God's specific direction to be a part of His activity in reaching a specific people group or a specific city or country. God's call to individual churches often comes in one of these forms as well.

Multi-site is about following God's leadership related to reaching people in specific communities. With this focus, multi-site churches notice lifestyle and behavioral characteristics of the people they seek to understand.

Larry Ali, executive pastor at Desert Vineyard, describes their community: "Forty percent of our community commutes to Los Angeles to work. We're kind of like a bedroom community. And so we feel like people don't want to commute to church. That's the kind of indicators we've gotten, and so if we can keep church close to the people, that's going to be an ideal situation."

LifeBridge is in a different state but has identified a similar need. LifeBridge is located in Longmont, Colorado, in Boulder County. "We've always been sort of a regional church," said Dan Scates. "A lot of people commute to Denver or Boulder to work and then come back into the smaller communities. They also commute to our church from these smaller communities.

"In a way that fits our culture. These folks like to go to downtown Denver and watch the Broncos, watch the Nuggets, but come home to smaller schools, smaller communities. And so in a spiritual sense we thought we could tap into that and do the same thing. LifeBridge's multi-site strategy is to "take a worship service and outreach into the smaller community and yet allow them still to have access back to large events—youth events, women's events, retreats, and different things like that"—at the original campus. These new sites allow LifeBridge to "service those communities and provide a closer proximity for outreach."

Stepping beyond commuter communities, some multi-site churches are reaching into rural areas. Pastor Keith Boyer pointed out that the majority of Crossroads Community Church's campuses are in rural communities. Churches in "smaller communities aren't going to grow unless there is an anomaly or an exception to become a size where they can afford some of the staffing and benefits of a larger church. That is one of the tremendous advantages of being multi-site for us in a rural area.

"Rural communities are able to experience something as a video campus that quite frankly a church even of two hundred would have a challenge to finance as far as quality of children's ministry, staffing, teaching . . . everything that we are able to offer."

Multi-site churches are not only located in commuter cities and rural areas, but also urban areas of small cities and large cities. When a church's sites target different types of people, this is more difficult. They must experiment and invest in listening to the people in the community.

Don Ruppenthal, associate pastor at RiverTree Christian Church, described their experience as they started two new sites. "What we have found is that even twenty minutes away in each direction, the cultures change so much from where this site is. The other two sites are different. They are just totally different, which is kind of amazing."

RiverTree asks, "What's the X factor of the community you are going into? What is that thing that makes it different? There are differences in every one of them, and you want to find out what that is that will get you the inroads—that will get that trust going where they will actually come and visit."

How Location Interacts with the Core Group

Boyer described the heart of the core group as Crossroads added their first new site. "To a person around the table they were saying, 'I can't wait to launch this campus because there are people that are near me that are far from God that I'm going to be able to get to come to church now.' And that is exactly what has happened."

Northland, A Church Distributed has learned to seek to get to know their core group. This starting point allows them to answer the strategic question, "Where can we have the greatest impact for service?"

Northland's focus has shifted from simply needing space to looking for the potential of what God can do through the layleaders in this new location. Executive director of worship Tim Tracey summarized their new outlook: "We are much more focused on how can we serve and how has God equipped us with leaders that maybe are currently driving all the way to the Longwood campus, but they would be unleashed if we could support them in their community where they are."

Start a Site Where Your Church Already Is

Growing churches like Northland draw people from greater and greater distances. This distance discourages these members who fit your church from inviting those around their home to your church. This is latent potential for further word-of-mouth growth through personal invitations.

Christ Fellowship Church launched a new site in a former Target store in Royal Palm Wellington. They literally had a couple thousand people attending their Palm Beach Gardens campus at least semi-regularly who drove from this community. The length of the drive limited their participation to just on the weekend. As these people yearned for more midweek things close to them, it was natural for Christ Fellowship to choose this area to launch a site. Dave Lonsberry summarized their goal: "We are basically trying to be very strategic in terms of the locations, like a lot of other churches, so that we can be closer to our people so that they can more effectively minister in their area."

Teaching pastor David McKinley described Prestonwood Baptist Church. "We're a regional church and we have people from everywhere you can imagine coming. But with the continued growth north of us, we really felt that we are beginning to have members who are living a distance where they are going to drive to come to church, but they are not going to bring their neighbors. They are not going to bring their families. They are not going to be as engaged."

As Prestonwood began looking at a site nineteen miles north of their original campus, they realized "we had two thousand members who by zip code live in an area about ten to eleven miles north of the existing Plano campus." While the site they chose was further north to reach some brand new communities, there was a large base of people close by to help join this launch.

If You Can Read This, You Are Too Close

Several churches who started sites within a short distance of their original campus found it was difficult to get the core group to "stick" at the new site. Many people are eager to help get a new site started, as it represents an exciting new ministry to them. However, it becomes easy to opt-out of this ministry a year later when there are more activities and options available at the original campus.

"I think our proximity killed us," stated Joey White, campus pastor at First Baptist Church McKinney's north campus that is located about four miles from the original Louisiana Street campus. "We were too close, and we probably misjudged the desire of our people to jump at a contemporary worship model as well as a new discipleship model in small groups. . . . We had a Gideon moment. God really pared down that number to a core group of about one hundred twenty."

Mike Miller, director of ministry support at Community Presbyterian Church, can understand the difficulty of making the new site "home." He described those involved in their second site that is six or seven miles from the original site in Danville, California. "If you already drive [to the original campus] two or three times a week for other classes, it's just too easy to drive down on Sundays."

It is essential for the core group to buy in to the new site as their church home, not just a temporary place of service. Choice of location is a key contributor to shaping this mentality.

Too Far Cripples Critical Mass

Creating a critical mass of leaders who have regular responsibilities at the new campus allows the new site to start from a healthy position that is poised for growth. Without critical mass, any growth that is realized is used to backfill positions and really is not going to move forward until positions are filled. When tasks don't get done, your new site will miss opportunities to reach new people, welcome them appropriately, and make the necessary connections with them.

Locations that are far from your church's current base of leadership will lack this critical mass. Your launch will be smaller, and size alone will make the site function very differently than your original campus.

"It would have been a huge help to have people who understood how Northview functioned and worked to come here on a consistent basis," said Robbie Stewart, campus pastor of the West Lafayette campus of Northview Christian Life Church. "We were supposed to have a lot of people from the main campus, and it just didn't happen. And that's not a slam against the main campus or anything. It just didn't happen because we are an hour and forty minutes away. People weren't driving up."

If you are selecting a location that will not allow a critical mass of current members to move to the new location, keep your expectations in line. You will find it much harder to generate momentum at the new campus.

Location as a Paradigm Shift

I can still hear the clunky, out-of-tune piano as we kids in the Sunday school department shout-sang, "I am the church, you are the church, we are the church together. All of God's people, all around the world, yes we're the church together!"

We got the point. So much so that we have felt guilty a thousand times since then when we caught ourselves referring to the church building as "church." Yet we are also a generation that has grown up doing church as if church is inextricably linked to a church building. While the church building paradigm has been helpful and supportive for tens of thousands of congregations, that doesn't mean it is the only paradigm.

Another great next generation multi-site insight came from Mark Batterson, pastor of National Community Church. "I went into church planting with the traditional mind-set: Meet in rented facilities until you can buy or build a building."

National Community Church was meeting in the movie theaters in Union Station in Washington, D.C. Batterson noted that about twenty-five million people pass through the station each year, and the station has a food court and access to the whole metro system.

"Meeting at Union Station just was a paradigm shift, because we realized how effective it can be reaching unchurched and dechurched people when you are in the marketplace." Batterson recalled, "It was a few years into it that we realized, 'Why would we build a church building when we have got a Union Station?' So that really transformed our perspective.

"For people who are unchurched, it can be a little uncomfortable or a little unsettling thinking about going into a church building. But when you meet in movie theaters, it is a very nonthreatening environment for someone to come in and be exposed to the gospel."

This vision for meeting as a church in the marketplace to hopefully reach the unchurched is part of National Community Church's identity.

One day, walking home from Union Station, Batterson "had this vision of us meeting in movie theaters at metro stops throughout the DC area." Batterson knew who his church was, and the multi-site vision was a perfect fit.

They now have locations at movie theaters located near other metro stops. They also took marketplace ministry seriously by launching a location in a large coffee shop. The coffee shop is a well-run business throughout the week and a place of worship on the weekend. Batterson points out that Jesus hung out at wells. "Wells were natural gathering places in ancient culture. And we just think that coffeehouses are post-modern wells."

The identity of National Community Church is closely tied to location. While your church needs to reflect your own identity, keep in mind that location is not as cut-and-dry or as rigid as you might think.

Multi-site needs to be seen as a way to do things that could not be done otherwise. Once a church begins to view location as a means rather than as the end, the doors of opportunity are wide open.

Choosing the Facility

With this perspective and a target community in mind, your church will be looking for a place to meet together. Key decisions include choosing the type of facility and deciding whether to rent or own a facility—in the short run and the long run. View these decisions as part of solving the problem of reaching a community, and choose a solution that is in line with your church's identity and values.

Here is a partial list of different types of facilities utilized by new sites:

- Movie theaters
- Schools
- Dissolved or disbanded churches
- Churches—meeting at off-peak times

- Community center
- Warehouse
- A former Target store
- Performing arts center
- Mall
- Coffee shop

Rental challenges

The most common challenge mentioned by multi-site churches was the challenge of functioning in a rented location.

Here are specific challenges they faced:

- Setup and tear down create a lot of wear and tear on staff and volunteers
- Lack of availability of on-site storage
- Getting the rental agreement and specific commitments in writing for the future use of space
- Rising or unpredictable future rent creates a large financial risk
- Lack of availability of a custodian or maintenance person when needs arise on Sunday
- Insufficient electricity to power the sound system requiring the use of generators
- Inability to secure high-speed Internet or satellite for video feeds requiring the use of DVD technology
- Lack of availability of the facility for anything midweek
- Limited rental options at the edge of a city's growth
- Finding a building with a sufficient number of parking spaces
- Lack of availability at prime Sunday morning times

God's Activity in Selecting a Location

"God picked that place," Guy Melton said of Oasis Church's North Miami location. "He opened the door. As long as He continues to open the door and show us that that's where He wants us, then I'm going to go through it. I would rather be there than where I *thought* would be our next place."

There are times that God leads a church to move into a location that is difficult. When an area has spiritually hard soil, the expectations of that campus must reflect that. For Oasis, their move into their Hollywood location meant redefining success. "There's not a doubt. It's a very tough place because of the urban environment. If you look at the other urban churches around us, we had to refocus. Success wasn't necessarily having a thousand or two thousand in the Hollywood campus in the first ten years like we did at Pines. It might only be in the hundreds. Consequently we have one hundred fifty to two hundred people and probably 50 percent of those have been saved since we started the church. That's an incredible thing!

"I'm more excited to have one hundred fifty to two hundred people with twenty being baptized than I am to have eighty baptized a few weeks ago from the Pines campus," Melton continued. "This is because we are reaching a very difficult place, but we are seeing life change. And we see the long-term incredible potential for downtown Hollywood."

Not only will some locations be more difficult, they also may require different expressions of their ministry. Oasis had to learn how to do ministry in an urban environment, and Melton admitted they are still learning how to do that.

The advice in this chapter helps you understand important factors in selecting a location. However, the "right" location comes down to being where God wants you to locate your next site. Once you see God leading, you need to understand the people in that community, and your planning should reflect the dynamics of that location that make it easier or harder for your church to minister.

CHAPTER
EIGHT

How Do You Communicate Multi-Site Effectively?

O nce leaders have approved the addition of a new site, planning begins in earnest. In the midst of the myriad of decisions we have begun to examine, communicating these plans may seem like an after-thought. However, if is far too important for it to lag behind. Key elements of good communication surfaced throughout our interview with three of the leaders from The Chapel. For this reason I asked copastor Scott Chapman to share how they communicated as their story rapidly unfolded.

Scott Chapman

copastor, The Chapel

Riding a Movement of God

Growing up in the Midwest I've never had much of an opportunity to surf. I've often imagined what it would be like to feel the ocean surge under my feet, lift me skyward, and carry me on the ride of my life. I'm told waves like that are rare. They can't be manufactured or controlled. They can only be ridden.

God is kind of like that too. Christians, like surfers, spend long stretches of time paddling through uneventful waters prayerfully waiting for a sign that God is ready to move. And, like a wave, a true movement of God can't be made or managed. It can only be ridden.

Over the past few years God has stirred the waters of our church and taken us on a thunderous, adrenaline-fueled ride that has widened our vision, deepened our passion, and changed us forever. It has been an exhilarating, unpredictable, messy, amazing, grace-filled adventure.

We began to feel the wave in March 2004 when we moved into our first permanent building as a church. We had seen God consistently bless and grow us up to that time, but nothing we'd experienced could prepare us for what lay ahead. In our first two weeks in our new facility, we grew by more than 130 percent in attendance, and in the course of the first year, we helped nearly one thousand people become part of God's family.

Three things stood out to us from that year. First, God was on the move and He wanted us to move with Him. It was clear to us that God wanted to reach people who don't normally come to church in bigger and more profound ways than we had imagined.

Second, while we were reaching people who had never personally connected to God in an eternally significant way, we were not reaching people who didn't already believe in God. When we researched the spiritual condition of the greater Chicago area, we were amazed to find that nearly three quarters of the people who live here believe in the God of the Bible, yet only seven percent of them attend an evangelical church.

As we explored this phenomenon further, we discovered the dominant form of religion in our area was something we came to call practical atheism: believing that God exists while behaving as if He does not. It is a faith that is so far removed from a person's everyday life that it makes no practical difference.

The dominant form of religion in our area was something we came to call practical atheism: believing that God exists while behaving as if He does not.

Third, we realized that our rapid growth had changed the relational dynamic and overall health of our church. While our ministries were growing and many people were committing their lives to God, we found that our size made it more difficult to help people enter into community with each other and establish a pattern of life with God that would yield personal transformation. Our people were taking the first steps toward becoming an audience.

In a short time The Chapel had grown to more than four thousand people, and we believed that God was calling us to reach many more. We were already out of space in our new facility but were hesitant to build a large addition. We worried that an even larger crowd would make it more difficult to connect people relationally. We saw practical atheism feeding a growing disconnection between a passive church experience and the active, vibrant Christian experience that God calls us to enter and uses to transform our lives. How could we continue to grow in number the way God was leading us, while simultaneously increasing the relational connectivity and faith ownership of our people?

The answer God led us toward was to become a multi-site church. When it became clear to us that it was possible to combine the excellence, visibility, and ministry horsepower of a large church, the relational warmth, personal shepherding, and active participation that characterize a small church, and the connection to the broader community of a neighborhood church, we realized a new paradigm of church was born.

We anticipated that such a foundational change in the way we did church would represent a challenging transition for our people. We began our discussion with them through a weekend series that highlighted the reality of practical atheism and helped them form a more complete picture of what it means to follow God individually.

Toward the end of the series we explored with them the responsibility that we felt to continue to reach out, as well as deepen our experience of biblical community and spiritual formation. We invited them into a spiritual process that focused on discovering God's future for our church that culminated in a moment of corporate prayer where we as a church committed ourselves to the adventure of following God into a bold yet unknown horizon.

We did not use this series to introduce multi-site as a solution but to frame the challenge we faced and engage the hearts of our people in a spiritual process with God, trusting that He would begin to lead them. We felt that presenting the solution prior to exploring the problem would have removed the context for change. Additionally, we had no idea how to transition into becoming a multi-site church or even where we would start. We needed time for our leaders to get their arms around what it meant to take this journey with God.

During this time God profoundly moved. He brought four potential new campuses into view. A small Lutheran church in our area was struggling to survive. Without knowing about our exploration of multi-site, they asked if we could help them turn things around. One suburb over, a nondenominational church with whom we had a relationship had plateaued and was looking for ways to have a greater impact in its community. Upon hearing about the possibility of The Chapel going multi-site, they expressed an interest in joining with us and becoming one of our campuses. We also learned that a church in a nearby city had moved into larger facilities and was selling its former building. Finally, around the same time, the Chief of Corrections of our local county jail who also attends our church heard we might be launching Chapel campuses and asked us to begin one in their facility.

All of these potential campuses came to us in the span of one month after we as a church had prayerfully committed to follow God into whatever bold adventure He had for us. We were both amazed and overwhelmed by God's provision. As daunting as launching four sites at once seemed, we were confident that only God could have orchestrated our circumstances.

Now we faced the challenge of leading not one, but multiple churches with different backgrounds and perspectives through the process of becoming one multi-site church. Many fears confronted our people during this time. They were afraid of losing some of their identity and uniqueness in this new blended church. They feared they would have to share their senior pastors with other congregations. They feared they would have to experience video teaching. Mostly they feared change itself.

We needed to help our people move past their concerns and embrace a selfless vision that served others they did not even know. We believed that we could preserve some of the uniqueness of each church, improve their pastoral shepherding experience by installing campus pastors over each congregation, and help them significantly experience the presence of God through quality video teaching. (People's fear of video teaching is always far greater than their actual reaction to it.)

The size of the task mandated that we embark on the largest and most complex communication campaign in the history of The Chapel. We began by crafting a central message that focused on the capability of multi-site to help us continue to grow rapidly while dramatically improving the quality of everyone's church experience.

We reminded our people that moving forward was not a new direction but the next step of a spiritual process that God was clearly blessing since its initiation some months before. We put together materials that cast vision, answered questions, and allayed fears. And, because my wife and I had recently adopted a daughter, we used the concept of a blended family brought together by God to frame the discussion.

After the central message came together, we began to meet with influential stakeholders from each prospective campus. We included staff, small-group leaders, ministry leaders, significant donors, and relational networkers. We processed the transition with them until the vast majority was able to positively represent the new vision. From there we began the process with the broader congregation. We designed a weekend series and held town hall meetings at every campus to introduce the idea and answer questions.

Then a week or so after the town hall meetings ended, we launched a campaign of home meetings to further discuss where we believed God was leading our church and provide everyone an opportunity to relationally connect with their campus pastor and me. Around this strategy we built a platform of Web postings, e-mails, and downloadable documents. We continued an informal dialogue with our people throughout the first year of transitioning into multi-site and ended the year with a final series of town hall meetings designed to help us remember all that God accomplished in the past year, as well as put to rest any lingering issues that still concerned them.

No process is ever perfect, and ours certainly had its successes and failures. And, no transition will bring everyone into the new work that God wants to do, no matter how much we may desire it. Yet, we were able to follow God into an exhilarating ride.

Over that next year we saw God expand that formerly Lutheran church of fifty into a campus of nearly six hundred, grow the plateaued nondenominational church from eight hundred to more than fifteen hundred, established a core of more than three hundred in an empty facility a city away and launch a campus for inmates where lives are transformed every week. God didn't just increase our church's attendance—He grew our hearts as well. People began to connect and grow on every campus. One indicator of the activation of our people's faith during that year was a church-wide 55 percent increase in the number of volunteers, the largest in our history.

We set out to help people rediscover the transforming reality of God in their lives; somewhere in the process I rediscovered the transforming reality that God brings to ministry.

Sharing the Vision

The motivation and the movement of God were evident in most of the multi-site churches we interviewed. The moment the leaders of these churches realized God was moving and they were tempted to try to just hang on was also the moment at which they needed to be sending clear signals to their congregations to catch the wave.

Exhilarating—yes. Difficult—you bet.

First, your single-site congregation will need help seeing the vision that your leadership sees. Parts of the message won't sound very appealing, such as changing their outlook on church and investing in a part of the church that will not directly benefit most of the current congregation.

Second, church members who have the courage to move to the new site need to understand the vision. They need to know the vision for this new site so well that when they explain it, it is the same as if the pastor were saying it.

Third, communication must begin in the community that your new site is going to try to reach.

Multi-site churches who have had communication success and failure provide practical advice for this important dialogue.

Sharing the Vision with Your Single-Site Church

"The harder thing for us to communicate vision-wise is that we are really a church that is focused on others," said David Parker, senior pastor of Desert Vineyard Christian Fellowship. "Communicating that vision is the greater challenge, more than just being a multi-site congregation."

If a church is already on board with a vision to reach others and serve others, they will simply see multi-site as another means to reach that goal.

"It scares me that some people are doing [multi-site] because it is the thing to do now. It's almost the cool thing and that's dangerous. I think that's a little scary," Mark Batterson, pastor of National Community Church, warned. "I think one key is that you have got to make sure that you have buy-in from your congregation. . . . The way we gauge that is with our surveys. If we had a survey that came back and said twenty people wanted to be part of a launch team, we are not going to launch that location."

Obtaining this buy-in requires continual communication.

"I have to, as senior pastor, be able to cast vision on this all the time," explained Steve Tomlinson, pastor of Shelter Rock Church.

From the perspective of Shelter Rock's original site in Manhasset, going multi-site hurt them. Tomlinson explained, "They lost leaders because they went to Syosset. Their friends that they used to have lunch with after church, they now go to Syosset. It actually was a little painful to make that move, and if you don't sell the vision as to why we do what we do, it is going to fall apart."

Jason Cullum, lead pastor at Christ's Church, put it this way: "You have got to sell your central campus or your sending campus on what the concept is, because this campus is actually paying a lot of the freight for the satellite campuses to start. So they have to understand what they are also participating in and get everyone involved in the process, not just, 'Hey, those people across the river.' That really creates the 'us versus them' mentality. But say, 'Hey, this is all of us as a church deciding that we are going to reach this community, and here is the way that we are going to do that.'"

Cullum indicated Christ's Church did the best they could with this communication, but there are several things he would do differently knowing what he knows now: "We would do a whole lot more video, a whole lot more pictures. I think it would become more of a regular topic that would be communicated on a regular basis. We did things on our Web page and did things here and there, but it was always the second tier communication pieces and we didn't do primary communication from the stage very often."

In hindsight, Tomlinson sees some key events that facilitated the adoption of the multi-site vision among key leaders and the staff at Shelter Rock. Churches in Long Island tend to be less exposed to what is working among evangelical churches across the country. Very little Christian radio is broadcast in the area. Very few conferences venture to their area.

A year after becoming their pastor, Tomlinson took all the elders and all the staff to California for a weekend. They did not go to attend a conference, but to visit real churches "to see what they actually pull off on a weekend." Their weekend tour included North Coast Church, The Journey, Mariners, New Song, and Saddleback. The result was that his leaders "saw what they never dreamed possible."

"If that trip had not happened," Tomlinson continued, "I think for me to try to explain one church, multiple locations would have been like talking Greek.

"When I got back here, my chairman of the board who comes from a Brethren [church], very 'fundy' background, was looking at the bar across the street from church and saying, 'Hey, they aren't open until 12 noon. Do you think we could have a venue there?'

"You know, they were thinking outside the box. And when we started talking multi-campus, they knew the vocabulary. They weren't caught off guard."

Henderson Hills Baptist Church also took a practical step to communicate. They made it a point to give the new campus pastor for the new site "face time" at the original campus. Owen Nease remembers, "I had a chance to share my story and how Amanda and I came to Stillwater. I think giving the campus pastor the chance to do that at the primary or the first campus is an important thing to do because that helped cast the vision."

As Mike Brisson, senior associate at Cornerstone Community Church in California, described their communication process, he revealed several things occurring simultaneously. They focused on the current step in their multi-site journey: the ninety thousand people who needed to be reached. They emphasized the longer term, bigger picture: "God has called us to the entire Temecula Valley." And they communicated a long-term commitment: "It's not just something we are doing short term. We have long-term plans there. We look to acquire property and build a building and have a long-term presence down there."

Communication Plan Example

Christ Fellowship utilized a very intentional communication plan as they went into multi-site. One reason it was likely more structured is that they also were seeking to raise money necessary to fund the growth. Amidst the spiritual focus of the process several communication principles resemble those often used in capital campaigns.

Dave Lonsberry, executive director of business and finance, described the process they used in 2004. "There was a lot of very intentional things done to instruct our people, to provoke them in a spiritual way to be sensitive to God's leading, to remind them of the goodness of God and what He has done through a very humble group of people that started in a living room twenty years before, and to see what God can do if people just commit themselves to God's ways."

Late Fall: 40 Days of Experiencing God

"We took the book *Experiencing God*, broke that across the six or seven weeks, and had our people go through that with us. That book speaks very much in terms of, 'if you want to really understand where you are to be, look for where God is working and pour yourself into that.'"

Winter: 40 Days of Prayer and Fasting

"We told our people, 'Hey, we are going to be sharing some amazing, important things about the future of our ministry after the beginning of the year. We want you to be in prayer during this time to prepare our hearts for where we are to be going for the future so that our pastor can be very clear with this and can effectively communicate what God is placing on his heart in terms of a vision.'"

January: Twentieth Anniversary of the Church

"We talked about everything that God had done in His faithfulness and His provision in those twenty years." The following weekend, the pastor began to share the vision for moving forward.

January–February: Vision Casting

"That was a six- or seven-week process where the pastor shared the vision." The vision was twofold: (1) maximize the ministry impact of our original main campus in Palm Beach Gardens and (2) purchase twenty acres to the east on which they had a long-term plan to build a new campus.

"The financial piece was actually a very, very, very small piece. We hardly even spoke about that during the weekend. We really focused our people on a spiritual mission to reach our region for Christ. . . . We were calling our people to give of themselves fully in every way so that we could have the impact that we are called to have.

> "We did follow-up messages in terms of 'why are we doing this?'
> and what the Scriptures are telling us in terms of why we should get
> involved. And then we called our people to a commitment to be a part
> of it."
>
> The financial piece was handled primarily in small and medium-
> sized group gatherings with the pastor. Over three or four weeks,
> seventeen gatherings were conducted for the church family in which
> the pastor shared the vision and people had an opportunity to ask
> questions.
>
> ### Fall: First New Campus Launch in Wellington

Chuck Carter, pastor at First Baptist Church Windermere, advised, "Vision, vision, vision, vision. Whenever you are sick and tired of talking about it, your people are probably just slowly starting to get it."

Sharing the Vision with Church Members Who Will Move to the New Site

Christ's Church used the following process: sent letters and called all the families in that area inviting them to an open forum meeting to talk through potential possibilities. Church members in the target area were brought in early in the process, since the leadership of the church wanted input from those in the area before they made a final decision.

To build awareness and interest, Nease set up an information kiosk in the lobby of the Edmond campus of Henderson Hills Baptist Church. He was able to interact with people as they gathered and went into the services.

Mark Batterson points out the reality that these volunteers need to understand about a launch. "Each was pretty

> *Vision, vision, vision, vision. Whenever you are sick and tired of talking about it, your people are probably just slowly starting to get it.*

exhausting just physically. . . . But my take is in the parable of the talents, the reward for good work was more work. It is more work. I think part of multi-site is just embracing this . . . this is going to be harder and that is just part of life."

Christ Fellowship chooses a location where they already have a solid base of attendees who can form the leadership. "But, we don't go there for those people," Lonsberry asserted. "We are very explicitly saying *we are not going there for you.* We are going there so that you can participate more in church life. Even more importantly—the evangelism piece—we want you to be able to bring your neighbors and friends to church with you."

On a practical level, Christ Fellowship planned several events for those who would move to the new campus. "We had a worship encounter in the school a couple months before it launched. We had a big picnic. We did a lot of things to try to develop some momentum in that area before we launched. And we did that in a highly relational way," recalled Lonsberry. "We tried to connect people and let them have a sense of when we're coming and why we're coming. We allowed them opportunities to hear directly from our pastor updates on what's going on."

> *We are not going there for you.*

Lonsberry described it as "an inclusive approach to the people of the area. So it's not 'Christ Fellowship coming'; it's we are all coming to minister in this area. And it fostered a real sense of teamwork and ownership among not just our staff, but our laity as well. . . . That was a huge deal for us."

After the launch Cornerstone Community Church has invested in weekly communication and time together for those who made the commitment to help with the new site. "We try to meet with all the volunteers before the service starts," explained associate pastor Mike Brisson. They give a CD of the sermon to those who are working in areas such as children's ministry who won't be in the worship service. "I am constantly casting that vision and telling why we are there and the importance of what we are doing and having kingdom impact and how it wouldn't be possible without their participation. It is kind of like a contributor service. It is a mini service just for them with a couple songs of worship and a short devotion."

Attracting People from the Community to the New Site

By far, word-of-mouth is the primary means multi-site churches use to attract people to a new site.

Robbie Stewart, a campus pastor for Northview Christian Life Church, said, "There are a group of people here who are just advocates for what we're doing and they invite a lot of people."

However, some multi-site churches supplement this with advertising. They specifically mentioned mailers, in-theater and newspaper advertising, and printed invite cards.

"We really put a lot of weight on the shoulders of our people," said Jason Cullum. "We said, 'Now it is your time. You said you had friends and people you would invite. Now go out and invite those friends. We gave them the tools, and they definitely jumped out and began inviting people."

Community Presbyterian Church in northern California has taken a number of marketing-type actions to build awareness about the new site, such as giving out hot chocolate on the street. They have also done "driveway drops" of invitations at Mother's Day, Father's Day, and Christmas, and they have mailed postcards.

Beyond awareness, Community Presbyterian has sought to do more relational things, rather than waiting for people to come visit their church. They have offered movie nights with free popcorn and soda. They have also worked with some soccer groups seeing an opportunity when a large new soccer field opened nearby.

As some multi-site churches found resistance in the communities of their new sites, they discovered some key elements of communication they had omitted.

Crossroads learned at their White Pines campus that renting an office did more than move the two staff members twelve miles from their Freeport campus. Campus pastor, Chuck Babler, explained the importance of the office. "We have a presence in the community all the time. And that was a big plus. I think it also started the growth. It made us more of a permanent fixture, plus we were able to be available in the community for people."

Don Ruppenthal, associate pastor of RiverTree Christian Church, shared another example of resistance. "They don't accept other schools or other people when they move into their community. It takes a long time for you to become a Massillon person. So we found out the hard way: (1) our pastor was not living in Massillon, and (2) his children didn't attend the school system, and (3) we didn't have that during-the-week presence there at all, as far as being involved in the community and things like that."

The Words You Use

My son Max asked to be excused from the table one evening. I told him he needed to eat the last bite of quesadilla on his plate first. He responded with the insight and wit of a clever five-year-old. "That's not a bite, it's a big crumb."

Max had nuanced a word knowing that the outcome of being excused from the table hinged on it. After laughing long and hard at his ingenuity, I insisted it was a bite. So he ate it.

Similarly reactions of those who hear multi-site being communicated will hinge on the nuances of the words we use. Sometimes words can communicate unintended meaning. The words and names for each site should reflect the location and not imply value. The following words should be avoided because they imply an order of importance: main, mother, daughter, satellite, primary, first, second, and such.

Dave Lonsberry added that Christ Fellowship "had to get over the hurdle of sometimes communicating multiple messages, some of them specific to a campus that weren't necessary for the whole church." They had to invest in "creating avenues of communication so that we can try to be very clear and not have a lot of clutter in our communications to people that don't attend that campus." Otherwise people would respond, "I don't need to hear that information."

Marc Cleary and Dan Ohlerking admitted that communication was a bump that they experienced at The Healing Place. "Communication is so important. . . . We make sure you don't devalue any one campus or overvalue any one campus. Making sure when you plan something that you keep all those different communication strings in your mind in doing that."

A quick example of how this simple principle is applied at Oasis Church is, "There is no main campus," pastor Guy Melton explained. To people, "their main campus is where they are at."

What Has to Change within Your Staff?

Initial Staffing

Initial staffing of sites varies across multi-site churches.

Stillwater Campus of Henderson Hills Baptist Church in Oklahoma

At its launch, the staff included a full-time campus pastor and a part-time worship leader who also led student worship at the Edmond campus on Wednesday nights.

Syosset Campus of Shelter Rock Church on Long Island

Initially hired a part-time teaching pastor and a full-time campus pastor. Over the next two years, Shelter Rock added a campus pastor at their original Manhasset location, hired a part-time children's director for Sunday mornings at Syosset, and shifted from a full-time youth director to two part-time youth directors—one at each campus.

Polo Campus Crossroads Community Church in Illinois

The only paid staff was a full-time campus pastor and a full-time administrative assistant. For the first year, half of the campus pastor's salary was paid from another part of the budget, because he still had some duties that benefited all of the campuses. This was mainly done for financial reasons, as they would have preferred for the campus pastor to be focused on the new site full time.

Temecula Campus Cornerstone Community Church in California

The initial paid staff included a campus pastor, a senior associate pastor, a part-time nursery coordinator, and a part-time children's worker. Cornerstone's associate pastors are generalists, so this was not their only responsibility. The campus pastor also oversees the recreation ministry and the missions ministry for the entire church and oversees the grounds for the main campus. The senior associate pastor oversees the campus pastor at Temecula, as well as the church's youth pastor, small group and women's ministry director, and an associate who leads adult Sunday school, senior ministry, and guest ministry.

Each New Campus LifeBridge in Colorado

The only paid staff members for LifeBridge's new sites are the campus pastor and a part-time children's pastor. LifeBridge utilizes volunteer leaders for all of the other ministries.

Fleming Island Campus of Christ's Church in Florida

As Christ's Church sent sixty to seventy families to start the campus in a local school, their initial staffing included a full-time campus pastor, a full-time worship leader, and a children's ministry intern. As the weekly challenge of setting up and tearing down continued, their next addition was a part-time tech person to lead the team that handled these duties.

Newberg Campus Evergreen Presbyterian Church in Oregon

Evergreen Presbyterian did not hire anyone initially at this campus. However, pastor Nathan Lewis shares that some of the part-time staff they have hired over the first three years should have been hired right away. "In about a year and a half, we have burned out members of these four families who were part of our original congregation, because they were eager to get this thing done." At that point Evergreen Presbyterian hired four part-time staff "to do certain tasks that have a high gift mix or to do tasks that no one likes to volunteer to do."

As Evergreen Presbyterian illustrates, decisions about adding staff after the launch tend to follow "pain points" or natural progressions of moving people from part-time to full-time.

Christ's Church wasn't the only church to add a tech person shortly after launching. RiverTree also realized this was needed both because they are not in a high-tech area, and they needed someone to oversee the setting up and tearing down each week.

The most obvious example of a church that hired to fill a necessary hole is Desert Vineyard. They did not have a campus pastor for their Tehachapi site for the first two years. They then added a full-time campus pastor. Over those first two to three years, they also added a part-time children's ministry director, a part-time bookkeeper/administrator, and a part-time project manager.

Another example of hiring as a church reached a pain point was Community Presbyterian Church. They are known at their original campus for having excellent children's ministry programs. As they sought to reach young families, they struggled to reach the same level at their new Tassajara site. So they hired somebody to lead children's ministry at their Tassajara campus.

Key Principles

1. A campus pastor should be the priority in terms of hiring.

2. You can leverage volunteers in key roles, but be careful not to burn them out.
3. The number of paid staff is usually related to attendance.
   - The expectation of large initial attendance based on a critical mass of members who move to the new site may prompt more hiring.
   - When the long-term expectation for a campus is for large attendance, the initial staffing is higher.
4. Be faster to hire extra help as you move beyond two sites, because your staff is already stretched and they know how much work it will require.

An important aspect of communication relates to hiring. Initially current staff members of the original church are called on to pull a little extra weight. Jason Cullum, lead pastor of Christ's Church, indicated that it is critical to help the staff to understand that this is a process. More staff will be hired, but it will take time. Managing hiring expectations is just one example of the importance of communication among the staff.

A "Matrixed" Organization

It is not hard to show an organizational matrix as Dave Ferguson did in chapter 4. However, it is much harder to answer the endless list of potential responsibility questions that begin, "Who is responsible if _____?" Some of these have become clear as you read about the campus pastor and core leaders, but others won't emerge until someone asks. Begin now to write down the answers to these questions. It will help you clearly communicate responsibilities as people are recruited or hired or trained. Knowing who has the authority for each ministry and how much autonomy each leader has is critical.

Stovall Weems, pastor of Celebration Church, explained, "When you get into that matrix-style leadership, it presents some new challenges and it forces you to raise the level of maturity and leadership and teamwork. When the leader is right and the leader is about team and it is about the whole, then overall it really raises the quality of leaders in your church."

Dave Lonsberry, executive director of business and finance at Christ Fellowship, explained a matrix environment. "What that typically means is that if you are a pastor or staff person in a particular function at a particular campus, you are accountable to your campus pastor first, but you are also accountable to the leader of that function for the whole church that happens to maybe be back at the [original] campus. You've got a dotted line back to them."

A matrixed organization creates new communication challenges. "Now, all of a sudden, you have a couple different bosses that you are accountable to. So what that really requires is a high level of coordination and communication between those two leaders, the core director [of that function] and the campus pastor." They must anticipate how things will impact other people.

Lonsberry explained the tangible ramifications. "We had to change our meeting structures—who was in the room at what time—so that people were more in the loop earlier on, because otherwise you are getting drawn and quartered if you're a down-line staff person and the two different people are asking you to do two different things and you are responsible for making both happy."

David McDaniel, director of North Point Ministries at North Point Community Church, spoke frankly about this. "All churches that have done this . . . end up with some kind of matrix organization . . . which is just confusing."

As a church gets ready to answer how they are going to make all this happen, "It's just an excellent opportunity for Satan to get in and divide a church staff. I mean it's just a layup." McDaniel summarized, "You can prescribe how we're going to handle all this, but without a huge amount of trust and mutual respect and prayer, the opportunities to split are just everywhere."

Proactive Communication

Joe Stowell, teaching pastor at Harvest Bible Chapel, illustrated the stress multi-site places on a staff. "It's been hard on our staff morale. We have staff spread out over five campuses, so people don't see each other as much anymore and the relationships aren't quite as tight."

Keith Boyer, pastor of Crossroads Community Church, shared how he addresses this relationship and communications challenge. He conducts a weekly meeting with all the campus pastors—either in person or a conference call. In addition to this meeting as a team, Boyer contacts each of them individually each week.

Beyond his personal interaction with the campus pastors each week, Boyer emphasized, "The communication link between the campus pastors and central support team is huge." Typically Crossroads has a monthly meeting for this purpose, but they also encourage communication to occur as often as necessary.

Campus pastors at Crossroads typically meet twice a month with champions, the volunteer leaders of each ministry. Chuck Babler, campus pastor at the White Pines campus, has individual meetings with the champions at his campus quarterly.

The importance of communication in a multi-site church can be seen in where multi-site churches invest in staff members. Two roles that several multi-site churches have seen the need to add are a minister or director over communication and a technology director or chief information officer. Dave Lonsberry explained that Christ Fellowship is "making some pretty significant investments in creating tools necessary for people to be able to do ministry and keep people connected that way."

Roles Change

As soon as a church adds a second site, staff members that previously led ministries for the original campus add a second job description. They still lead their ministry at the original campus, but now they are a central support leader for both campuses. For many churches that primarily utilize volunteers as core leaders of ministries at the new campus, this staff member also inherits a third job description. They are the staff member leading their ministry at the new campus.

Needless to say, multi-site is more work. Such multiplication of duties is only possible when the ministry leaders can find and equip layleaders through whom to multiply their ministry. A middle level of leadership is essential. "Middle-level" leaders are those between the staff members and volunteers. These leaders allow you to have multiple teams within a ministry. Staff members who have not been cultivating and investing in middle-level leaders will struggle with the multiplication of roles.

"The bottom line is you can't just subdivide your one person. You have to have team members," said Steve Tomlinson, pastor of Shelter Rock Church.

If growth continues and more sites are added, these roles eventually will be staffed separately. Each ministry will have a dedicated leader for each campus and a leader for the ministry across campuses. Typically, this is a multi-year journey. So, your staff members must be invested in the multi-site strategy to make this personal investment of wearing multiple hats.

Probably the biggest shift that occurs is in the role of the senior pastor. Dave Browning describes the shift: "I ended up working less *in* the ministry and working more *on* the ministry. It sounds real easy to make that shift, but if you love pastoring and you love people, giving away

> *I ended up working less in the ministry and working more on the ministry.*

ministries and pastoring the pastors—which is what I have ended up doing more of—is a challenging trade-off."

As Browning described the personal pain of making this shift as pastor, he shared a saying that they have at Christ the King: "There is no growth without change; there is no change without loss; and there is no loss without pain." As Browning modeled a willingness to endure this pain in his role, it solidified a culture of growth within his church.

Marc Cleary and Dan Ohlerking on the lead pastor team at The Healing Place, shared a similar shift in their pastor's role. They noticed that some of the bumps along their multi-site journey simply reflected the need for personal leadership development among the campus pastors. Lead pastor Dino Rizzo responded by investing everything he knew into these campus pastors.

> *There is no growth without change; there is no change without loss; and there is no loss without pain.*

"It really is important we make sure we create these times for the campus pastors to meet with the pastor." Cleary and Ohlerking have noticed the fruit of this investment. "As a result you'll see a closer unit. You'll see the communication is better. Whenever problems or issues do come up, you'll see it handled a lot better."

As pastors adjust their roles, they are modeling the flexibility that is required of staff members in a multi-site church. Cleary and Ohlerking said, "We have real good fluidity in our staff. Everybody knows when you wake up today, 'Hey, what you're doing today you might not be doing next week. You might be the youth pastor. You might be campus pastor.'"

Such fluidity could promote insecurity, but as staff members learn to be secure amidst the movement, it creates a very strong staff. They are better equipped to navigate challenges as they arise.

Phases of Multi-Site

Pastor Keith Boyer of Crossroads Community Church described the phases they experienced as they added sites.

Phase 1: Two Sites

"Your first [new] campus is exciting. It's like having your first kid. Yeah, it's a lot of work and more challenges."

Kevin Penry, pastor, operational leader at LifeChurch.tv, agreed. "Going one location to two locations, an organization doesn't have to necessarily change a lot to do that."

Pastor Larry Osborne of North Coast Church explained, "Creating the first one, because we had so much excitement, everybody's willing to take on a little more work. Creating the second or third, there's a little more hesitation. After that, you almost have a system down; for instance, we will hire extra help. We realize you just can't kill people."

Phase 2: Three to Five Sites

Penry continued, "By the time you go to the third location and beyond, you have to begin to adapt some real different strategies organizationally."

"Once we decided to launch a [third site]," Boyer recalled, "things really began to change. We had to do a total shift with our infrastructure, our staffing structure. The shift was such that it's not only a change in philosophy of how we do church but it changes who we are. We don't just do multi-site, we *are* multi-site. And that was a radical shift."

Pastor Dave Browning agreed that as Christ the King Community Church reached three sites, they were "just getting our head around the fact that we're not just meeting in one place anymore. So we have got to think about others, other sites, other locations." By the time a church has three sites, the entire mind-set of how to think about church changes.

Several multi-site churches used the same phrase Boyer used. They all realized that they were no longer just doing multi-site; they were multi-site. This not only reflects the staff members' changing roles; it also reflects a day-to-day change in how they think about decisions. The first filter for every decision is the effect on all the sites.

LifeChurch.tv was on the leading edge of the multi-site movement. They described moving from doing multi-site to being multi-site. However, they added a third step. They reorganized to multiply through multi-site. Not all multi-site churches choose to keep adding sites, but for those who do their organization must adapt for the next phase.

Phase 3: Five or More Sites

Boyer went on to describe the staffing need that emerged with additional sites. "We've had a lot of our strong staff members—who champion children's ministry, worship, student ministries, and adult ministries with small groups—end up taking on an additional job description as a central support team leader in addition to what they did at just the original campus for a number of years. So that really stretched some people. Now I'm trying to release them from some of their responsibilities at the original campus day to day, where they are actually able to serve the overall church at all the campuses and work with the leaders."

Dave Browning pointed out that growth from five to ten sites was a difference in style. "We couldn't just informally get information out anymore. We had to get it out more formally." Browning explained that with a few sites you would naturally bump into the other pastors and cover what you needed to cover. As Christ the King Community Church approached ten sites, they set up area pastors who could be responsible to communicate with the pastors in their area.

While many multi-site churches cannot relate to having ten or more sites, the principle behind area pastors is applicable in any size church. Browning explained that they use the term *span of care*. "We want our span of care to be real small so that we can stay really personally connected." What prompted the move to area pastors was the fact that a couple of pastors resigned when Christ the King had ten or twelve sites. They were not plugged in enough as Browning was trying to care for ten pastors at once.

At each stage of growth, a church needs to assess the span of care that each leader has whether they be caring for staff members or for volunteers. Growth requires constant organizational change to keep this span of care small.

Christ Fellowship also is adding separate ministers who are not tied to a specific campus overseeing each function. They began to move this direction as they planned their fourth site. The size of their sites (the smallest of the first three had one thousand attending on a weekend) prompted the need to make this move earlier than Crossroads.

> *We want our span of care to be real small so that we can stay really personally connected.*

Christ Fellowship refers to this new staff structure as a core model, with leaders for each function who are not attached to a campus. These functional leaders will drive the vision, strategy, calendar, and the creative work for their area of ministry for all the campuses. Executive director of business and finance Dave Lonsberry explained, "Their job is to think globally, because as soon as you have people assigned to a campus and trying to think globally, it just creates a challenge for them to try to do both.

"As we launched our third campus," Lonsberry continued, "especially for senior leadership to try to keep three campuses coordinated without someone at each ministry coordinating for that function, just added a lot of complexity to the management piece." While the need emerges with three campuses, most multi-site churches cannot afford to create such staff positions until either these sites grow or as they continue to add sites.

What Can't Change

As a multi-site church changes its organization, the roles of staff members, and adds new staff, one thing cannot change. Staff members must be deeply committed to the multi-site vision of the church. This prerequisite to becoming a multi-site church grows in importance as changes occur.

As staff members spread out across campuses, it is imperative that the vision and message about who your church is and where it is going does not get diluted. Lonsberry pointed out the importance of making sure staff do not "allow themselves to get too centered on what they are just doing on their campus to be able to understand the big picture and be brought into that. That's super critical, because if you have people pulling in different directions, it's just very inefficient. It tends to hinder everybody in some form or fashion."

Dino Rizzo, lead pastor of Healing Place Church, shares more of their story to reinforce the culture within the staff that is necessary in a multi-site church.

Dino Rizzo

lead pastor, Healing Place Church

At Healing Place Church, we have learned a few things about the challenges that being multi-site brings. In 2004 we added our first two multi-site locations, and in the next four years we added seven more.

On the surface no two campuses look alike. One of our campuses is in a rural area, with mostly long-time residents who love to hunt and pretty much all know everyone else in the community—and all their aunts and uncles and cousins, too. Another campus is in a community in the heart of one of the poorest zip codes in the United States. We have a Spanish-speaking campus reaching a huge-and-growing segment of our community. There's another campus on the other side of the country in a community that is comparatively

---

wealthy, and two others are on the other side of the world, smack in the middle of African communities dealing with the AIDS pandemic and abject poverty. Each of our other campuses is equally unique in one way or another.

With such a diverse collection of cultures that our campuses are serving, it would be absurd to think we could be effective as a church if we tried to force everything to look exactly like it does at another campus. Some of our campus pastors wear goatees, some shave clean, some shave their heads, some work a little spike action. Some of the team members tuck their shirts in, other go tails out, and others might even wear a tie once in a while (and yeah, they get looked at funny when they do). We decorate the mirrors in the bathrooms in one way at one campus, and another way at another campus, and maybe not at all at yet another campus. There are simple things that just make each campus unique. And that's OK because we don't only reach out to one type of community or demographic, so we do our best to ensure that a campus takes on the flavor of the community it serves.

But even with all their differences, beneath it all, there is a God-given vision and core DNA that guides Healing Place Church—we are a healing place for a hurting world. We work hard to keep this heartbeat by being very aggressive and intentional about reminding our team that this is our one mission as a church. Every campus, every staff member, every leader, every ministry must reflect that mission.

As often as possible, we pull our campuses together for combined events and outreaches. We hold many of our all-staff development meetings on location at various campuses, always making it a priority to communicate what is going on at each campus to the team as a whole. We do life *together* and we enjoy being with each other. A testimony that comes from a changed life at one campus is something every other campus celebrates.

Likewise, a challenge at one campus is a challenge for all the other campuses. That's how it works around here: *We celebrate each other's wins, and we hurt with each other's hurts.* There is great value in our staff and leaders having a three-musketeers attitude: "One for all, and all for one." We aren't competing with each other to see who has the best campus or who gets the biggest slice of the budget for sound equipment. The focus is not on us and our needs, but on people who feel lost and forgotten in the world today. We are one team that is just doing all we can to show hurting people the love and healing of Jesus Christ.

It is easy to see that a staff that serves in so many varied cultures could, over time, grow further and further apart. So we encourage our team—from the campus pastors to the finance office staff, and from the children's team to the video crew, and everyone in between—to continually remind themselves that *we are all a part of something that is much larger than we are by ourselves.* And that means that when one of us speaks, acts, writes, designs, types, greets, drives, mows, edits, paints, sweeps, or answers the phone, we are representing the whole team—all campuses included.

There's a principle in this that we call "presencing." Each of us has to be able to effectively *be* the presence of one another; to "presence" one another. When one campus pastor stands to say something, he is responsible to represent the whole team (the other campus pastors, the rest of the staff and leadership, the lead pastors, the nursery workers, and the parking team—*everyone)* in every word he speaks. It isn't about "me and mine" but "us and ours." It is as simple as dying to self—a plain old laying down of our own desires, agendas, and ambitions in favor of the good of the whole body.

At home I often remind our kids that if each of us will just look out for the best interests of the rest of the family, everyone will have their needs met. This is how multi-site church works as well. The more that mind-set soaks into all we do and say, the harder it is for one campus to lose sight of the tremendous value of every other campus. That is where the "all for one, and one for all" mind-set thrives.

This doesn't mean just giving a nod to the fact that another campus exists—it is actually *preferring* one another. It means serving each other. This is the way God's economy works. If you give up your life, you'll find it. If you give, it will be given to you.

Long before HPC went multi-site, we had been doing all we could find to do to embrace other churches—striving to be a church with a kingdom mind-set—not just a Healing Place Church mind-set. Now, in the same way that we want our campuses to remember they are part of a bigger picture. We cannot be healthy with a "fish-tank" mentality, where we think that where we are is all there is. The kingdom of God is *huge*.

> *Each of us is a unique, well-painted, well-crafted piece of a large mosaic, which when it is completed must spell out "JESUS."*

Each of us is a unique, well-painted, well-crafted piece of a large mosaic, which when it is completed must spell out "JESUS." And, when it is all said and done, we know that we are only as valuable to the kingdom as our ability to reflect Christ to those around us—reflecting Him as He washed the disciples' feet in John 13.

We are at our best when we do not allow it to be about ourselves, and instead make it always all about serving others in Jesus' name.

Leadership Development

I am dumbfounded at times to think of the concentration of resources God has assembled in the United States:

- **Believers**—Yes, it can be discouraging to see this concentration diluted in recent years, but the number and percentage of evangelical believers in the United States is historically remarkable.

- **Technology**—For God to put the concentration of believers in the country that is leading the world in creating new communications technologies is a greater blessing than we could ever ask.

- **Knowledge**—Advances in technology have coincided with our ability to accumulate, access, and search knowledge. Many in the developed world have come to virtually worship the idol of knowledge by trusting it to meet their current and future needs and to solve their problems. However, we also have unprecedented access to biblical knowledge and teaching. (What did people do before cross-reference Bibles?)

- **Wealth**—Consider the concentration of wealth that has occurred in the United States since World War II. Never has a nation been so blessed materially.

- **Transportation**—Growing up at the United States headquarters of WEC International, a missionary sending organization, I daily spoke with retired missionaries whose journey to the mission field involved taking a ship overseas. The traditional sojourn of four years on the field and one year at home for furlough was necessitated by the time and expense of travel. Today we think nothing of sending church members to the other side of the world for a mission trip. Their entire investment of time would have been spent on a ship never reaching their destination if this were attempted sixty years ago.

- **Time**—Never before has a society had so much discretionary time. We don't seem to notice, but our busyness has nothing to do with scraping together food, clothing, and shelter. We are overloaded with recreational activities.

Investing Our Resources

We may look back at this point in history and realize that we have already passed the acme of these concentrations. However, each is still at an incredible level.

How has our generation invested what God has given us as a church in the United States? The parable of the talents refers to money with which the master entrusted his servants. Since any of the resources mentioned here could be given a price, the principle of this parable can be applied to any of these assets.

How is your church utilizing the people, time, technology, mobility, biblical knowledge, and finances with which God has entrusted you?

Look within your church; you will likely find that several people are qualified to lead each ministry in your church. Being a good steward of these resources means being proactive preparing and encouraging each of these people to take on new leadership responsibilities and asking others who currently stand watching on the sidelines to step up.

The church in Antioch was such a church. The level of teaching was exemplary. There were no less than five renowned prophets and teachers (see Acts 13:1–3). Yet God did not choose to open a seminary or conference center around these teachers. Instead He quickly sent two of them out, multiplying their effect on their world.

Multi-site churches intentionally multiply the resources God has given them. Yes, most of the opportunities have been God-given and not devised by church leaders. Yet, much like Antioch, God has given the churches the opportunity to multiply their effect on their world.

The most important concentration that exists at the churches that have gone multi-site is the concentration of leaders. Many single-site churches have the same concentration or even higher levels. Launching new sites forces multi-site churches to move people along in their leadership journey. This is a necessity when you launch your first new site. If you are going to continue the multi-site journey by launching more sites, leadership development must become an ongoing priority.

Teaching pastor David McKinley highlighted the stewardship principle that multi-site allowed Prestonwood Baptist Church to demonstrate. "As a church we weren't willing to just sit still and say, 'OK, we're big enough. We have done enough. We have got a great history. We have got a great facility. That's fine.'

> *The greatest thing is the strategic initiative of the pastor and the passion and commitment of the people to stay on mission when we really could have said, "We have done enough."*

The greatest thing is the strategic initiative of the pastor and the passion and commitment of the people to stay on mission when we really could have said, 'We have done enough.'

"And this really has been a breakthrough point for us, for our people. You talk about discovering leaders in your church! You didn't know they were there because they were kind of stockpiled. Just in the existing structure, we found people who stretched to embrace and serve and sacrifice and give."

> *You talk about discovering leaders in your church! You didn't know they were there because they were kind of stockpiled, just in the existing structure.*

Who Stays and Who Goes?

Ultimately churches are volunteer organizations, so the answer to who stays at the original site and who goes to the new site is "whoever wants to go to each." However, staff and church leaders have the opportunity to set expectations and to encourage particular individuals to move into the new positions of leadership at the new campus. When those positions are paid part-time or full-time positions, then you do have much more control over who stays and who goes.

So as you view your responsibility for at least influencing this decision, watch out. People are watching you. David McDaniel, director of North Point Ministries at North Point Community Church, described the situation.

> You're in charge and you've got three people. You've got kind of an A player, a B player, and a C player that are on your staff doing children's ministry in one site. Quick question: "Who do you send to launch the new location?"
>
> If you are kingdom minded, you just love this idea, you'd go, "Wow, this is a cool opportunity for my A player to really

stretch his or her wings and be the children's ministry person in the new location." Right?

But really you think, "Wow, you're already stretched really thin and you've got an A player that's doing not a third of the work but probably half to two-thirds of the work. You might say, "I could send my A player and then I am in trouble. So, I'm going to send the B or C player."

But the campus pastor knows who the A player is and so he's thinking, "Well great, I'm getting the leftovers."

McDaniel gave this hypothetical example, which can be applied to both volunteers and staff, to say that these kinds of decisions are potential areas of conflict and confusion within the staff and send signals to those who are considering going to the new site.

As the staff at my church approached potential leaders, particularly for roles in leading Bible study groups at our upcoming Mount Juliet campus, the first question they often heard was "Who else is going?"

We can make the argument that this is the wrong question. Even Abraham disobeyed in this area by bringing along his nephew Lot. Yet, it is a legitimate question for someone to ask who is leading the core ministries at your new site. It will say a lot about your church's commitment to the site if they see A players in core leadership positions.

Andy Stanley made such a decision as North Point launched new sites. Elaine Jones runs the Browns Bridge Community Church and she was one of the North Point founders. Jeff Henderson, who runs the Buckhead Church, was the most promising leader among the second generation of leaders at North Point. McDaniel pointed out, "Andy clearly made a decision: 'I'm putting A players in these responsibilities.'"

People Want to Step Up

Larry Osborne, pastor of North Coast Church, observed that "as the church gets large it tends to have a few all-stars do everything. . . .

Multi-site puts us back to those early days over and over where people are needed."

Keith Boyer, pastor of Crossroads Community Church, echoes this principle. "More people get in the game and serve with a sense of energy, passion, and purpose."

Osborne gave an example related to musicians. "You go to a lot of big churches and after three weeks you realize the bass guitar is owned by someone and you might be a bass guitarist, but there's no place for you. When you see the bands change in all the venues, you step forward and say, 'Wow, I can play.' So it actually helps volunteerism after a first little fright of how many more you need. Even the skill set is not as great; you know, to be the worship leader in a venue of four hundred is not the same thing as a room of four thousand. So from band members to children's and youth workers, smaller things need a little less skill set."

Osborne also observed, "All in all, volunteers volunteer for the task, but they stay for the relationship. So by keeping things smaller, you've got higher relationships."

From the pastor all the way down to volunteers in each area, the focus must be on ministry. When the focus is on ministry, then leaders will be equipping new leaders. Osborne challenged, "A lot of people talk about equipping, but they don't really mean it. You really need to mean that equipping is an important thing." For Osborne, giving away ministry means sharing the pulpit. For every level of leader this means sharing responsibility with new leaders who have a chance to gain experience.

Dave Lonsberry, executive director of business and finance at Christ Fellowship, indicated that this principle is what made their Royal Palm campus successful. Their approach going in was, "We want to involve the leadership and let them know that this ministry is theirs too. And they have got to help drive it. They have got to help lead it and they have got to help own it."

So, Christ Fellowship found that the ones who stepped up were motivated by the right things. They wanted to share Christ with their friends in the communities near the new site.

Don't Look for Perfection

Dan Scates, multi-site minister at LifeBridge Christian Church, pointed out, "Our philosophy is you're not going to find the perfect leader. You're going to have to get someone who will attempt to lead, see how they work out, and try and encourage that person. What has happened a lot of times is there is someone within the team that's really going to become the real leader."

This basic principle has worked well for LifeBridge at a number of levels. Scates gave an example on their set-up and tear-down team. The initial leader was really a good doer, but not great at recruiting a team of people to do the set up and tear down. As they saw another person on the team who had these skills, they gave him more responsibility. When the first leader stepped down, the second leader was ready to step in and became the leader. When a change at work caused him to leave, a third leader from within the team stepped up and has been the best leader for this team.

Scates summarized, "We don't seem to land perfect leaders right off the bat all the time." Scates noted it is important for the staff member to transition leaders in a ministry skillfully without losing the other people that are not being asked to step up. This constant leadership development is critical to the health of each ministry.

Often there are still positions to fill at the new site and gaps at the sending site. Dave Browning, senior pastor of Christ the King Community Church, described what happens as leaders move out to a new site.

Sometimes you tread water for a little while. Often it sends you out to look for the leaders that God has probably deposited in your ministry and you overlooked.

We have the 80-percent rule, which says that if we can identify someone who can do the job 80 percent as well as what we would wish for, then we should go ahead and go for it. Because we have found that the difference between 80 percent and 100 percent is not worth the effort and the energy that it takes to get there.

For your average person it does not make that big of a difference. The analogy we use is the ink jet printer versus the laser printer. Everybody knows the laser printer prints better, but pretty much everyone is OK with the ink jet printer. It's good enough.

Many of us were weaned on the whole "excellence honors God and inspires people" mantra. It's been an interesting journey for some of us to let go of that and to let real people do the ministry in a real way. . . . This is a story not really about how good we are. It's a story about how good God is and how He uses real people.

Browning noted that this could include having a worship center whose guitar player is pretty good at best. Most of Christ the King's worship centers do not use PowerPoint. They use overhead projectors. "We want to love people into God's kingdom," Browning concluded. "We're not here to impress them into God's kingdom."

We know from Scripture that God wants us to do our best in everything. Yet we also know from Scripture that in our weakness, God shows His strength. He works when we cannot. He goes further when we fall short. Christ the King and LifeBridge are not putting God to the test by finding the weakest people they can find, but they are also not putting ministry on hold waiting for a perfect leader.

Clearly Christ the King's model of church will not fit the model of church for many who read this book. Some of you listed "excellence" as one of your church values, and many of you haven't even exhaled after reading that a megachurch is using overhead projectors. Browning admitted that there are not a lot of churches following their model, and few people have studied what they are doing.

The principles expressed in chapter 3 still apply. You need to do multi-site in a way that reflects who your church is. Most churches shouldn't try to adopt Christ the King's organic model. Yet these same churches should pause and reflect on how tightly they are holding onto some of the expectations they have of who they are willing to move into the next level of leadership.

Who Is Responsible for Leadership Development?

Scates emphasized the value of the campus minister in filling volunteer leadership roles. "The campus minister sees what happens, sees who the leaders are, gets a sense and a feel for who might be a good leader on the team." The campus minister can then talk with staff members about putting these individuals into positions of leadership within their ministries on that site. "Without the eyes and ears and hands and heart of the campus minister at the site," Scates concluded, "the [staff member] here would be handicapped. So as a team, they're able to get the right leaders in place. . . . It's a real team effort finding great volunteer leaders."

Several multi-site churches pointed out the need to articulate up front how this relationship will work. Who takes the lead in putting volunteers into positions and in hiring staff members for a new site? While different churches do this differently, the two most important principles are:

1. Someone has to take the lead—either the campus pastor, the staff members over each ministry, or the leader over each ministry at each campus.
2. Work together as a team, valuing the strengths that each leader brings to these decisions. The campus pastor is in a unique

position to identify and meet potential new leaders and to see the week-to-week performance of current leaders. The core ministry leaders at each campus also are in a unique position to identify volunteers who are ready to step into the next level of leadership within their ministry. The ministry staff members have ministry-specific expertise that gives them a clear idea of the type of person who will work well within their type of ministry. They will also be responsible for training this new leader and equipping them to move that ministry forward at that new site. Training has a role in many multi-site churches, but it is usually specific to each of the different ministry areas.

At Celebration Church they have a volunteer coordinator who constantly is following up with people and getting them plugged into the life of the church. Pastor Stovall Weems indicated that leadership development is fueled by assimilation. "As long as we are assimilating people and we are getting people plugged in and involved, there's enough [leaders] to expand into these other venues and campuses."

Process

McLean Bible Church has started a Future Leader Program for interns. Director of community campus development Mike Hurt explained, "We're bringing in between six and ten interns a year to spend in a year-long focused training that has theological training and ministry training as part of their hands-on role in an ongoing ministry."

These interns provide practical help in each ministry, but they also help McLean develop future staff members. Hurt considers this a "must" for multi-site churches who will continue adding sites. "They have got to be developing staff and getting a pipeline of leaders."

Valley Bible Fellowship considers their leadership development their church growth program. It is organized around teams. Each team is comprised of a captain, three lieutenants, and five soldiers under each lieutenant. Teams are gender specific. Once a month the senior pastor gets the captains together and spends time with them. Every two months each team conducts a community service project. On an ongoing basis the teams are meeting for fellowship.

However, Valley Bible Fellowship was an exception among the multi-site churches we interviewed. Most were mobilizing leaders, but few have a well-defined process for equipping and developing leaders. Many were like Crossroads Community Church. Lead pastor Keith Boyer observed, "I think one of the greatest lessons we learned is in the area of leadership development. Honestly, we are sort of trying to catch up here. We launched four campuses in under three years, and part of that was intensified when we moved 1,000 miles away to really start a new church, which is an extension of our existing church."

Despite the lack of well-developed leadership development, most multi-site churches described the need for it. As we have described, the flow of leadership from the senior pastor to the campus pastor to the core leaders to other leaders within ministry areas at a site to volunteers is critical. Gaps or breakdowns in this flow will hamper the growth of new sites and make it difficult to keep sites connected.

A first-generation multi-site church that has a well-defined, well-developed leadership development process is Community Christian Church. Jon Ferguson has shared much insight through the NewThing Network and has kindly provided the key elements in developing reproducing leaders.

Jon Ferguson

community pastor, Community Christian Church

A Reproducing Church Demands Reproducing Leaders

When we reproduced for the first time with our Romeoville campus, we identified and developed a whole new cadre of leadership to launch that campus as well as backfill the places where leaders were leaving our existing campus to be spiritual entrepreneurs at this new location.

Four years later we launched our Carillon campus, targeting seniors in an active adult community just north of our Romeoville campus, and again it required reproducing leaders: artists, small group leaders, and ministry team leaders.

This past March we launched our Plainfield campus. We selected a target date, found a location, developed a marketing strategy, and chose service times. After all the planning was complete, it still demanded the hard work of identifying and developing leaders who would carry out the vision for this campus. Up to the last few days prior to the launch of that campus, our focus was on being sure we had leaders in place to successfully launch this campus.

We now have nine campuses with more than twenty-five celebration services at Community with an additional seventeen churches in our NewThing Networks. Every time we launch a campus, a celebration service, or even a church, it's all about *helping people find their way back to God*—that is our mission. But we know the only way we can accomplish that mission is when our leaders catch the vision for investing themselves in someone else who can also lead.

Currently there are thousands of multi-site churches in the U.S. And many more churches will become multi-site—that is, they will launch a new campus. However, there is a significant difference between launching a new location or campus and becoming a *reproducing church*. When it comes to a being a reproducing church—repeatedly launching new services, campuses, and churches—there are no shortcuts. It demands reproducing leaders. And we've discovered that every leader needs four key relationships in order to successfully reproduce again and again.

A Reproducing Leader Needs FOLLOWERS

This may seem obvious but is often overlooked. I can't tell you how many times I've thought, "This person looks like a leader, walks like a leader, talks like a leader," and placed him or her in a leadership position *before* he was put to the true test of attracting a following and being an apprentice, and I regret it.

There is a difference between attracting a *crowd* and developing a *following*. Crowds are temporary. They come and go. They're fickle and unpredictable. Followers are in it for the long haul. When Jesus enlisted His disciples, He drew them out of the crowd and challenged them to follow Him and do life with Him. Having a following is not the only test of leadership, but you can be sure if there are no followers, there is no leader.

Crowds Are . . .	Followers Are . . .
Temporary	Lasting
Fickle	Loyal
Unpredictable	Committed
Transitory	Consistent
Fleeting	Faithful

We have found small groups to be the best incubator for growing reproducing leaders because only a person capable of developing followers will be a successful small group leader. And if a leader has proven capable of developing a following in a small group, there's a good chance that one of those followers could be an apprentice.

A Reproducing Leader Needs APPRENTICES

We challenge every leader to have an apprentice—someone he or she is working with and developing in order to become a leader as well. There is a simple process for developing an apprentice that applies to any leadership role. It's based on 2 Timothy 2:2 where the apostle Paul writes the following to his apprentice Timothy: *"And the things you have heard me say in the presence of many witnesses entrust to reliable men who will also be qualified to teach others"* (NIV).

This advice Paul shares with Timothy reflects what Luke wrote about Paul in Acts 16:3: *"Paul wanted to take [Timothy] along for the journey"* (NIV).

Here is what it might have looked like for Paul to take Timothy *"along on the journey"* and what it could look like for a leader to reproduce him or herself in an apprentice. While there are many tasks and areas in which an apprentice needs to be developed, this process has proven successful for a variety of leadership roles.

- **Step 1**—I Do. You Watch. We Talk.
  If a person is leading a small group, for example, the apprentice would primarily observe the experienced leader as he or she leads the small group and then the two meet together regularly to discuss what was observed. This time of debriefing is crucial for a successful apprenticeship and needs to continue throughout the process.

- **Step 2**—I Do. You Help. We Talk.
  In this phase of development, the leader gives the apprentice an opportunity to "help" lead in a particular area. For example, if someone were being developed to become a student ministry

small group leader, the leader might ask that person to lead the prayer time, while the experienced leader leads the rest of the group.

- **Step 3**—You Do. I Help. We Talk.
  Now the apprentice transitions from assisting or helping to being the primary leader of the team or group. If a person was being apprenticed to lead a team of sound technicians, he or she would operate sound and provide leadership for other sound technicians. The more experienced leader releases leadership and now helps the new, developing leader.

- **Step 4**—You Do. I Observe. We Talk.
  The apprentice process is almost over now as the new leader is increasingly more confident in his or her role. Consider this process in children's ministry: In this phase a children's group leader would give his or her apprentice an opportunity to fulfill all the functions of leadership in a fail-safe environment with the more experienced leader looking on.

- **Step 5**—You Do. Someone Else Observes.
  This is where the process of reproducing comes full circle and the former apprentice is now leading and developing a new apprentice.

A relationship with an apprentice is a fundamental to a reproducing leader. However, every reproducing leader also needs the input and accountability of peers.

A Reproducing Leader Needs PEERS

In his book *Five Dysfunctions of a Team,* Peter Lencioni says the best form of accountability is "Peer-to-Peer Accountability." He says the healthy competition that is experienced among peers combined with the natural desire to not let them down makes it an ideal environment for leadership development.

Have you ever noticed that Solomon, the wisest man who ever lived, wrote more about the importance of wise counsel than all the other biblical writers combined? Think about it: Why would the man who needed it least recommend it most? Simple: He was the wisest man in the world. Wisdom seeks counsel (see Prov. 1:5; 12:15; 15:22; 19:20).

In our NewThing Networks we provide ongoing peer-to-peer accountability for church planters through reproducing networks. We are finding that this is one of the most attractive aspects of being in a reproducing church network.

At Community, reproducing leaders find peer-to-peer accountability in leadership huddles. Huddles are regular gatherings of leaders in small groups where they pray for each other and share wins, challenges, and best practices. These huddles are led by a coach, or leader of leaders.

A Reproducing Leader Needs a COACH

Developing a leadership layer of nonpaid coaches (leader of leaders) has long been a priority at Community. The temptation is to solve the challenge of caring for leaders with paid staff. Most recently we have put significant effort into this, realizing that in order for us to continue to grow, expand our outreach, and care for the number of people God continues to send us, we can't afford to pay enough staff to carry out this task of not just caring for people, but caring for leaders. Every leader needs a coaching relationship.

Our effort to develop coaches for leaders led us to create a new model for coaching.

At the heart of the model is a focus on "Relationally Driven Care." We have discovered that the one constant in a healthy coaching relationship is a growing friendship between the coach and the leader. Out of that relationship flows three coaching tasks:

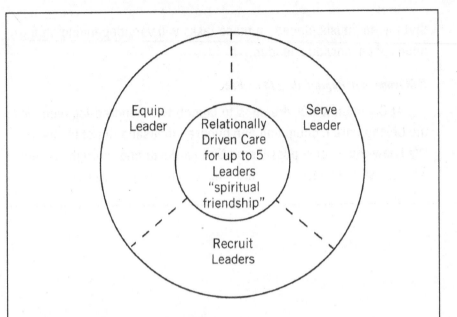

Equip
Leader

Relationally
Driven Care
for up to 5
Leaders
"spiritual
friendship"

Serve
Leader

Recruit
Leaders

Figure 7: Coaching Model

- *Equip*—It is the coach's responsibility to ensure that the leader is given the necessary tools and resources to be effective. This may come in a variety of forms including books, blogs, Web site, podcasts, training opportunities, and such.
- *Recruit*—A coach will provide guidance for the leader in identifying apprentices and team members or group members. Assisting a leader in identifying potential apprentices is one of the most important tasks of coaching.
- *Serve*—Occasionally a coach will need to come alongside a leader to do ministry together. This may be during a crisis or when a leader is experiencing personal challenges or is uncertain of his or her ability to lead in a particular situation.

Notice in the model that "Relationally Driven Care" is surrounded by a solid line to represent that it is the constant. The three tasks that flow out of that relationship are separated by dotted lines to indicate that the emphasis placed on these tasks will vary depending on the needs of an individual leader.

A Movement of Reproducing Churches

At Community our dream is to launch two hundred locations in the Chicago area, equipping one hundred thousand Christ followers. We know this is only possible as God works in and through leaders who invest themselves in others who, in turn, can lead as well.

Keeping the
Sites Connected

n contrast with most of our interviews, there was one interview that discovered many doubts—the anonymous church in chapter 2 that became a multi-site church out of compromise. Repeatedly through-out the interview, the staff member openly wondered whether the second site would remain part of the church.

With this interview fresh on my mind, I had dinner with a new friend from my church who was considering being a part of our third campus. He, too, wondered why our new campus would need our multi-site church after it was up and established, especially since we were planning on having live teaching.

Hearing these two sets of doubts within days of each other, I simply wanted to respond, "You just don't get multi-site."

Then I realized I don't "get" multi-site until I can articulate what it is that they don't get. Needless to say this didn't happen on the spot. In fact there were several leaders who had been at multi-site churches for several years who were still trying to figure this out when we talked with them.

Amidst their doubts, legitimate questions were asked:

- In name we are all one church, but what really makes us one church?
- Once a site becomes healthy, why should they remain a part of the larger church?

These doubts hinge on how one views multi-site and how one views their own church.

Scott Chapman, copastor of The Chapel, summarized, "Is multi-site a tech thing? No. Is multi-site about growing your church really big really fast? No. It is really about creating communities that are going to thrive. And being able to find a way to do things you could never do otherwise. And once you start to realize that, the door is wide open."

It is a tool to accomplish a mission. Some people will find this tool to be their favorite. Others will prefer not to use it. The leadership of a church must determine whether this is a tool God is leading your church to use.

As God leads your church to be multi-site, it becomes part of your church's vision. This vision had to be bigger than a single-site church. If the vision had fit within your original site's community or its space, you would never have become multi-site. Accomplishing this vision is why the sites need to stay together and work together. You can't reach the people you have set out to reach without each other.

It is a leader's role to articulate this vision and to keep the many parts of the church working together to accomplish it.

As your church unifies around becoming multi-site in its vision and plans, it also becomes part of the church's values. It is a value or a "must have" that will attract some believers and staff members and push away others. It sounds simple, but you have to want to be connected. Some people want to be part of a bigger kingdom venture or enjoy being creative together. Others want to be a pioneer or try their own ideas. Both can be innovative. Both can be effective. But these are two different values. Individuals need to decide if the vision of the church fits with what God is calling them to do personally.

Once your church understands that multi-site is a tool and is a good fit for who your church is, you will still need to be proactive in keeping sites connected.

How to Keep Sites Connected

Learning from the "Do-Overs"

When my son, Max, and I play one-on-one basketball in the neighbor's driveway, it is not uncommon for Max to say, "Let's start over." He never says this when he is beating me. But when I manage to take the lead, an instinctive voice in this five-year-old's head says, "The outcome does not look good. Let's pretend this never happened."

When Dave Lonsberry was asked if Christ Fellowship has had any "do-overs," he described some things they would do differently related to the launch of their Wellington campus if they could.

> We sent our teams out with a mentality of "you are going to be pioneers. We want you to break some new ground. We want you to try some things differently."
>
> That led to, for instance, the children's ministry out there being called something different with a different logo, totally rebranded. I think it was even a different curriculum. Student ministries, though it was the same brand, had a slightly different ministry philosophy. The worship experience was not too dissimilar, but it was different songs being sung.
>
> The coordination between the campuses wasn't as solid. And we really felt the sting of that when we went to launch City Place and it was yet a third thing. . . . And so all of a

sudden, it was like trying to manage three different churches. It hit us real hard.

In talking with other multi-site churches, Christ Fellowship learned that many of them had sought to standardize much of what they do. Within weeks of launching the Ascent worship services at City Place, Lonsberry recalls that their executive pastor, Todd Mullins, realized, "We have got to do what we do differently, because it is not manageable to have that many moving parts. We have got to be wise about where we allow variances and wise about where we say, 'Let's figure out the one best way and pour our resources into that and then just copy it multiple times over.'"

That is what Christ Fellowship did. They went back and realigned. "Now, we have the same children's ministry, student ministry, everything," Lonsberry said. "The lingo that we use, the jargon that we use is the same at all campuses."

The anonymous church mentioned in chapter 2 that began a site out of compromise has found it painful to reestablish a virtually broken connection between their two sites. The primary culprit for such a disconnect was how people were thinking about their church. A clear connection to a greater goal than one's local site was missing in the original vision and also was missing in the staff and laypeople.

A key staff member shared, "Ownership is a huge deal. You need to see yourself as a representative of the main campus, not as a branch of the main campus or an arm of the main campus. But you need to see yourself as a representative of the main campus, that you really are a part of a specific church. You are just meeting with people on another site. I think how you view yourself is pretty critical."

His advice was to answer key questions on the front end. "Do we have a clear vision, and do we know what success looks like? And if we don't define that ahead of time, then you start getting all kinds of interesting questions. You would probably get them anyway, but at least you could go back to the original goals and say, 'No, here is what we agree on.'"

This missing shared vision is what haunts this church's multi-site efforts. When present, this shared vision is what keeps the sites connected.

Systematic vs. Thematic

Multi-site churches use different methods to keep people heading in the same direction. Some do so very systematically. Others do so thematically.

Christ Fellowship chose to move to a more systematic means of keeping their sites connected and moving in the same direction. North Point Community Church is another example of a church that has systematized things to support their vision. In fact, North Point requires churches or church planters to use their ministry model if they are going to be a partner. David McDaniel explained, "It's not that we think it's the best model in the world and that everyone ought to convert over to it. It's just the only one we know how to coach. . . . If it gets hybridized, we don't know how to coach any more."

Despite the use of best practices across sites, McDaniel also pointed out that as a ministry plans to pass along programming that has worked well at the original site, they need to think through how well it will work at the other locations. Does the new site have the people to make it happen? Do they have a facility that is conducive to this program?

Chartwell Baptist Church in Oakville, Ontario, provides a sharp contrast. Executive and missions/outreach pastor Jim Carrie admitted that because Chartwell has given their sites a lot of autonomy they were still debating and seeking to articulate what it is that holds them together. The easy part of the discussion is "the financial, the administration, the behind-the-scenes stuff, because none of the sites want to take on property insurance, budget preparation, technical support. Each congregation was very happy to have a group in the center looking after those."

In addition, Carrie indicated, "We have a much stronger missions program because we are multi-site, because we could afford to hire people to lead our missions program and to do adult missions trips, youth mission trips.

"There is actually something bigger that is even more important and also at the same time less tangible—the sense of working together on our teaching, working together on our youth, working together on our children and family ministries." In the end Carrie concluded that it came down to the value they share of working together. The strength of the vision and values of the church is what keeps their sites together even without rigid systems in every ministry.

Oasis Church is an example of a church in between the thematic and systematic extremes. Oasis has nonnegotiable aspects of their church that go across all sites, such as having the same vision, philosophy, mission, and core values. Oasis has the same names for ministries and the same style of worship at all their campuses, but the ministries organically are allowed to develop their own personality. They are resourced similarly, but this, too, is not rigid.

At Oasis, community groups must be trained like the original campus except for variations caused by where they meet. For example, they have found it harder to find homes to meet in at the downtown location because there is a large variation in the wealth of those who attend. Those with nice homes are afraid to bring in some of the challenged people and the homeless. Outreach also varies by location. Downtown does block parties with the chamber of commerce and parades with the city on the beach. Those type of opportunities are not available near their suburban campus.

How to Keep Sites Connected—Mind-set

Each individual in a multi-site church must choose to put the kingdom of God first and seek to be a part of the way their church is participating in kingdom advancement. If an individual's mind-set shifts toward herself or himself or toward a ministry or group or site, it weakens the cooperative work of the whole church.

Your site is not your church; it is your venue for worship and your mission field.

Your ministry is not your church; it is your means of service.

Your small group is not your church; it is the people with whom you build community.

Your multi-site church is your church.

Nathan Lewis, pastor of Evergreen Presbyterian, articulated the vision within their identity that acts as the glue across their diverse campuses. These sites are in very different settings and have different styles of worship. "I would say that the DNA is that we are mission minded. We are committed with our dollars and our strategy to multiply congregations for worship; not only PCA congregations, but evangelical congregations. We're desperately underchurched, so part of the DNA is that everyone is more than willing to work hard or tolerate at least a church multiplication strategy. We have to do it or no one else will."

How to Keep Sites Connected—Technology

Multi-site churches that utilize video list a number of technology challenges. Many of these we have not addressed, because both the problems and the solutions are changing so rapidly. In terms of staying connected, the following principles should stand the test of time:

Northland, A Church Distributed learned the hard way how valuable it is to utilize standardized technology. Keep in mind Northland's delivery method for teaching is the most challenging: concurrent worship. At one point Northland had five different technologies connecting their sites. In the words of Tim Tracey, executive director of worship, "That was crazy."

Northland standardized their technologies so that if equipment fails they have backup units.

A second principle comes down to one profound statement from Barry Smith, pastor of Impact Community Church: "Mobile is a whole different animal." The optimal sound and technology setup has to be built from scratch (often re-created weekly) whereas the original campus is in a stable location and crafted over time.

It is important to try to avoid specific references to sites, times, or days that may remind viewers that they are not live or could even be perceived as indicating that they are not the intended audience. However, mentioning each of the sites is a way to remind all the sites that you are a multi-site church.

How to Keep Sites Connected—Teaching

Churches that utilize a single teacher across sites, usually facilitated by video, place a lot of emphasis on teaching as the glue. Tim Tracey said, "The sermons become the convening force for the vision of what God's doing at this church."

Larry Osborne, pastor of North Coast Church, agreed. "What should church be is really communicated as the Scriptures are taught. It's the communicator that sets the tone for the values and the way people think about church." Even though North Coast has several different venues that exhibit polar opposite styles such as Edge and Traditions or Country Gospel, "they hear exactly the same message. So we haven't had any sense of kind of becoming two different churches at all. I mean literally zero."

Mark Batterson agreed but also saw a need to share this responsibility. "As we grow a little bit larger, we are trying a hybrid where we are going to have our different point pastors or campus pastors preach and have a little bit of a preaching presence, because I'm also concerned that it's the person preaching that tends to be viewed as the pastor."

At the other end of the spectrum, Cedar Park Church is a church that does not have a single teacher across their sites. Each site has its own teaching pastor, and they do not rotate. Senior associate pastor

Craig Gorc explained, "Because it is not inherently connected through a central communicator, the tendency is that churches become disconnected. The strength of the structure comes down to the relationships of the individual leaders at each particular location."

Similar to Cedar Park, Upper Arlington Lutheran Church has multiple people preaching, with live preaching at all services. Their numerous services and venues also include a wide range of styles. The ministers get together a couple weeks ahead of time to talk about each upcoming sermon. They preach the same Scripture text and seek to be consistent in the direction. Brodie Taphorn, community leader and one of those who preach, indicated, "Even though we have consistency in what we are saying, there is some diversity and some contextualization as to how we say it." The stories and the lingo will be quite different in a Gen X service compared to a traditional service.

How to Keep Sites Connected—Music

By far, the most common approach to keeping sites connected in the music portion of worship is to use the same worship plan or order of service at each site. The style, instrumentation, or arrangements may differ in some multi-site churches, but it is very common to not only be teaching on the same topic but to be singing from the same music.

A handful of multi-site churches take this a step further. Churches like Northland, A Church Distributed, LifeChurch.tv, and Christ Fellowship Church seek to have many of their services simultaneously singing the same songs.

Dave Lonsberry, executive director of business and finance at Christ Fellowship, explains, "We all start at the exact same time for the exact same song at one time with live worship bands at each campus. So we sing the first song together in unison and what you are seeing on the screens are shots of the stage at each campus . . . so you are seeing that we are all together, one church worshipping at the same time."

While Christ Fellowship does not keep the live feed throughout the service, they are usually back online for the message with the ability to time delay it. In contrast, Northland keeps the entire service concurrent.

With so few multi-site churches trying to have simultaneous or concurrent music, it is clearly not a necessity to keep sites connected. However, these churches do catch a visual glimpse of a small portion of God's omnipresence, allowing Him to be personally present for the worship of millions of believers around the world.

On the other extreme, some multi-site churches must adapt what they want to do musically because the skill level of musicians across campuses is different.

How to Keep Sites Connected—Congregations

Pastor Nathan Lewis of Evergreen Presbyterian described several practical steps that they take to connect sites.

- We regularly pray for the other sites.
- Our leaders speak up front, telling exciting stories about what God is doing at other sites.
- In our worship bulletins, we plan three sections of announcements so that people can see what is being announced at other sites to encourage people going to different midweek events.
- We also highly encourage people to go and visit Sunday worship at other places, especially in the summertime.

Oasis Church realized they had not done a good job with this early on at their original campus. Pastor Guy Melton pointed out that the people at the original campus were the people "that are doing the printing, that are doing all the data entry, that are answering the phones, and even in the ministry areas we had not brought them enough into the process of the third campus. So, we have had to really work on that where we have tried to keep them better informed." Melton listed the ways they have done this:

- through our blogging;
- through our story-driven Web site;
- we have brought them down for lunches and meetings in the downtown area;
- we encourage them to come down and visit services;
- several staff members have been hired from the downtown Hollywood campus;
- every month and a half, our Hollywood campus worship team comes out to the Pines campus and leads worship, and our Pines campus worship teams will go down to Hollywood.

Melton concluded, "We're trying to set up different intersecting points of light for them to have to intersect. And we really, and this word is very important, we have to be *intentional*. And we weren't intentional enough at the beginning."

Pastor Steve Tomlinson of Shelter Rock Church wisely observed that when a smaller, dying church merges with a multi-site church, they often "have a low self-esteem." He added, "There is often a tendency for them to feel like 'we are not important.'" Even when nothing is intended, they may pick up on something and take it as an indicator that they are not important. Tomlinson shared several ways in which they have sought to prevent that:

- immediately investing about $350,000 to refurbish the entire church building;
- we make sure that we have elder representation from both campuses;
- we invested $13,000 in a playground for children right outside, in the very front and center to attract people with kids who were missing among attendees;
- alternating worship leaders, since one is especially gifted.

"You have to be proactive on that kind of thing so people don't feel like they are chopped liver," Tomlinson advised.

Stillwater campus pastor Owen Nease listed a number of big church-wide events that Henderson Hills Baptist Church does together:

- Student camps
- The big Christmas production
- Women's conferences
- Men's retreats

"We are using those as avenues to stick together," said Nease. Henderson Hills also created healthy circulation between campuses in a number of ways:

- Teams of volunteers from the Edmond campus would regularly go the Stillwater campus to help kick it off.
- Our small groups have been signing up for Sundays to come up to Stillwater and visit and see what's going on. And that has created some excitement.
- The elders from Edmond have been trying to spread their time up here in Stillwater. . . . They are making sure they come up and serve as pastors and servant leaders for the campus up here. The same thing goes for the deacons as well doing that.

The Healing Place also is intentional about making everyone aware that they are one church in many locations:

- campus pastors speak in midweek services at other campuses;
- mission trips for one campus are supported financially by other campuses, and video footage is shared at all campuses following the trip;
- "One Way" worship night with all of the campus worship teams together leading worship and prayer;
- two vision nights a year;
- a staff retreat each January that includes staff from all campuses, including those overseas in Mozambique and Brazil;

- video announcements to make sure each campus knows what the other campuses are doing.

Crossroads Community Church has improved over time in doing things to link campuses:

- an annual event the last few years has been the B3 Party, which is beach, barbecue, and baptisms bringing all the campuses together;
- five times a year, we call it MVP event, which is mission, vision, and purpose for our core ministry leaders;
- we do an annual Dream Team Celebration where we celebrate those who consistently serve;
- weekly e-news highlights different things we have done in the last week that we can celebrate—all campuses get the front page;
- common curriculum is maintained for their Kids Link program across campuses, including some video teaching.

Joe Stowell, teaching pastor of Harvest Bible Chapel, pointed out an interesting difference between sites that should not be overlooked: "Sometimes the spiritual temperature is different on every campus."

The previous weekend Stowell was on three different campuses on the same Sunday. "Every campus was listening to the same message and did the same worship package, but every campus felt different." Stowell explained, "Churches are sort of like an organism. Everybody is in a different place sometimes. And so what's a great worship package in one place may not be in another."

The challenge becomes constantly assessing the spiritual temperature and keeping your eyes open for spiritual problems or discouragement that need to be addressed. The goal, as Stowell pointed out, is for all the campuses to be "at a really hot spiritual temperature."

How to Keep Diverse Sites Connected

As you begin to think as a multi-site church, you will begin to consider the dynamics of each campus as you make decisions. The first step toward beginning to think this way is to notice the differences. Some of these you will know before you launch, and others will emerge as the group who attends regularly emerges.

Some basic demographic differences that multi-site churches have among their sites:

- Size of site
- Marital status
- Inner city compared to suburban or rural
- Different languages
- Different states
- Different countries
- Age of attendees

Brodie Taphorn quotes the pastor of UALC, Paul Ulring, describing the diversity of their sites and venues: "We have become a community of communities."

Multi-site churches who use video teaching have a particular challenge when they have diverse sites, because the single message must be communicated in a way that is relevant to these diverse locations.

Marc Cleary, on the lead pastor team at Healing Place Church, admitted that being one church that spans inner city, suburbs, and different language/ethnicity campuses is an overall challenge that affected "the way we plan the weekends, the way we plan the sermon series, and scheduling of events. All those things we really had to go through how we do each and every one of those things and make sure we're not thinking of just one or two campuses, but all the campuses, all the different environments."

Dave Lonsberry admitted it took many months for them to begin to make decisions and to begin to think globally first rather than making a decision for a campus and then wondering how it impacted the others. "Now on the front end of every decision, it's not even intentional anymore. . . . Just naturally we think about the impact on all the campuses."

Asking what a decision means for each campus before the decision is made has become a habit. It is a discipline. Christ Fellowship has learned to take this a step further, "to gain the input of those campuses as well," Lonsberry explained. "Sometimes you don't know what the unintended consequences are. So it has required a certain level of pro-activeness and some management skills and communication skills to gain consensus."

Lonsberry continued, "It really placed a high level of importance on our midlevel leadership in the church to make sure that they are communicating with one another, with the people within their function at each of the campuses, and to think globally first. . . . It was a paradigm shift."

As Harvest Bible Chapel grew, they also became more diverse. As their staff and elders conducted open lunches, they learned from their members who are African-Americans, Koreans, and immigrants from Iraq. Teaching pastor Joe Stowell recalled input from several Korean members. "They were like, 'Look, we want a voice. We want to feel like we are part of it. But we also know what kind of church we are going to, and we don't expect this to become a Korean church. We would love to feel that we are valued.' Little by little, over time, over the last couple of years it's just happened."

Valuing different ethnic groups took various forms. Translating services into Spanish and Polish was an obvious step for specific campuses. Starting a gospel choir happened naturally and has been a great thing for the church. By listening, Harvest Bible Chapel has gotten better at acknowledging and even celebrating different cultures within their services.

Avoiding the "Redheaded Stepchild" Syndrome

Pastor Mark Batterson was one of many who used the stepchild analogy. "Be really careful to avoid the stepchild syndrome. It is real easy to give all the attention and all the excitement to the new baby, the new location. We have really tried to validate our older locations, that 'Hey, you aren't any less important.'"

Barry Smith, pastor of Impact Community Church, also indicated that people can feel like the redheaded stepchild when they see most of the resources going to the main campus and not their campus. However, resources can mean more than just money. It can arise when they see less emphasis put on their campus. For worship teams, they can feel degraded if they are given less rehearsal time or are told to rehearse on their own rather than being led.

Not only do church staff mention the stepchild analogy, Jason Cullum indicated that in the early days of Christ's Church's first new site, "I heard that phrase thrown out a lot" among attendees. What did it take for that to disappear? It took investment in a new building and a great staff that fit the amount of people they have attending.

This investment in a new site can tempt even staff members to resent this use of funds when they have to tighten the belt in other places to accommodate. Shared vision and good communication are essential in avoiding such temptations.

Mike Ladra, pastor of First Presbyterian Church of Salinas, indicated that "probably the best thing we did was we didn't just build a new facility. We also improved the old facility [at the original campus], so that everyone in the church could give and were benefiting."

> ## CHAPTER TWELVE

Specific Types of New Sites

Two specific types of new sites deserve separate guidance:

1. starting an ethnic or multi-cultural site, and
2. merging with or absorbing an existing church.

Starting an Ethnic or Multi-Cultural Site

The fact that Healing Place Church has a Spanish campus today has more to do with plantains than anyone's plans. Mark Stermer, campus development pastor, recalled that things began with outreach that Healing Place was doing within the community through food distribution. "We would get 18-wheelers of different food. We ended up getting a load of plantain bananas, believe it or not. And so we said, 'What are we going to do with this?'

"We couldn't find anybody who wanted to take them, so we found a place that had some Spanish people living and we brought them in. They loved them. As we handed them out, we were looking around and saying, 'Man, this is a people group that is being taken advantage of.' They were in low-rent housing, and I just said, 'Lord, how are You going to start a church here or something?'

"And so God spoke right back to me. He said, 'Well, you start it.'"

Stermer didn't speak Spanish, and he had no answers other than recognizing the need. "I went to the home where we had given out the bananas and actually sat down with him and told him we wanted to do a Bible study. And it took me about thirty minutes to tell him that because I took a calendar, a Bible, and a clock, and I told him, 'On this day at this time,' and showed him my Bible."

That first Bible study had about fifteen people, and Stermer only had one person with him who spoke a little bit of Spanish. "It was the most horrible Bible study we had ever done. But we told them we were coming back. I was crying out to God, and the next week a guy called me that was actually a great interpreter who wanted to help."

From that Bible study the fellowship grew. They found a building, and Stermer continued to pastor there for a year while still working a job. After a year Stermer turned it over to the interpreter and his wife, Fernando and Missy Gutierrez. Healing Place stayed involved with this fellowship but only as a sister church.

After Healing Place began to launch new sites and understand the multi-site approach, they realized that this Spanish church would be a great fit within Healing Place. So they brought their leaders on staff and merged the finances. "We are helping them even more with resources. From there God just kept it flourishing and now we are in a new building and they are doing great." As we spoke, Healing Place was preparing to start a second Spanish campus.

If you consider starting an ethnic or multi-cultural site, first consider the need for initiative from the pastor, find the right campus pastor, and get to know the people.

Pastor's Initiative

"I think the most important thing is the senior pastor," said pastor Mike Ladra of First Presbyterian Church of Salinas. "He has to delight in different races. If he has any kind of hesitancy at all or has any kind of racism, it is not going to happen. He has got to delight in it, and that will come out in how he talks about it and how he leads his staff.

"Number two, the staff has to uniformly, without exception, delight in it, because if they don't, that too, will come out," Ladra continued. "I think everybody assumes this, but I really believe the staff every week has to pray for it. For a long time we prayed. I think a lot of this is the Lord answers that kind of heartfelt prayer."

Valley Bible Fellowship does not have a separate ethnic campus, but their sites reflect the communities they are seeking to reach. Their Bakersfield, California, site is about 50 percent Hispanic and includes a good number of African-Americans. Their Las Vegas site includes many Asian, African-Americans, and Caucasians. Senior pastor Ron Vietti put it plainly: "You know, I just minister to everybody the same."

Church of the Highlands was intentional about adding a site to reach the large population of Hispanics in their community. Blake Lindsey, campus pastor for the Riverchase campus, shared how it began. "Our senior pastor probably a year and a half ago just really had it on his heart to begin looking into the options of reaching out to this community. We follow the philosophy of waiting for a leader to emerge before we start something, so we began putting our feelers out and watching for that opportunity to arise with a leader that would actually lead that campus."

The Right Leader

Given the criticality of the campus pastor for any new site, the importance is even higher for an ethnic site. The ethnic site will face challenges that the other sites may never have experienced, and the campus pastor is the key to responding to those challenges in a manner that is consistent with the church's identity, values, and expression.

Church of the Highlands found just such a fit with Alex Solito. Solito had already been studying Church of the Highlands and their approach for some time before they began to explore beginning a site. Solito also was leading a new Hispanic church, so some leaders were already in place. As they came under the umbrella of Church of the Highlands, this leadership simply needed to be supplemented with some people who could show them specifics about the Church of the Highlands expression.

By understanding at the very beginning that Solito was on the same page in terms of the church's beliefs, vision, and values, the leadership of Church of the Highlands knew they had a good foundation on which to build. They hired Solito as the full-time campus pastor for the Hispanic campus.

As Healing Place began to serve the needy in the inner city, they learned you don't have to have color to reach color. The poor have a lot of needs. As you begin to serve them and reach them, they accept you fairly quickly. In the midst of this success, Healing Place sought to encourage this blending of races by hiring an African-American to be up front. The mistake they made was they chose a man that the community knew did not prove himself. The community rejected him.

Healing Place learned from this mistake, and over time good leaders emerged. Their staff in the inner city is now a majority African-American. Stermer points out, "You do want to try to look like your community. I am a believer in that when the opportunity is there. But you can't force it; you have to allow it."

Blake Lindsey summarized the importance of the campus pastor for an ethnic or multi-cultural site: "Find that leader before you go starting something. Having the leader in place to begin with is very, very important because then you have someone who is passionate, who has a heart for that, and you have got somebody whom God has gifted. Having a leader in place before you begin something is a huge advantage because then you have someone who is ready to champion that cause."

Knowing the People

Knowing the people you are seeking to reach is essential. For First Presbyterian Salinas, it impacted where they chose to build their new location. Ladra said, "I think we overcame an ethnic barrier by not choosing a site outside of town that would have been in a wealthy area. We chose to stay in town when we built, and that helped us a lot."

First Presbyterian also knew they were targeting second- and third-generation Latinos. This meant that language was not a barrier and as "a few Hispanics started to come, it really was explosive growth because they come as extended families. So once it started rolling and they found us to be very happy and accepting and found the staff to be very warm, then it was explosive growth."

In contrast, Mark Stermer faced a language barrier as he sought to start a work among the Spanish-speaking community that accepted the plantains he offered. While God used Stermer's feeble attempts, it was God's provision of someone who spoke Spanish fluently, Fernando Gutierrez, which allowed the work to move forward.

By learning about the people you are seeking to reach, you will find out if the outreach can be mainstreamed as First Presbyterian did or if it will require ministry in a separate language.

You will also discover many cultural differences. Most of these are really not an issue, and you must be flexible with how you to take these into account. However, some cultural differences do not measure up to biblical standards. For example, Healing Place had to specifically teach on marriage, because they found that most couples who were attending were not married but living together.

Music is intrinsic to culture. "Latinos are just no different from us," Ladra said. "They choose a service according to the music they like." First Presbyterian benefited greatly from most of their worship band being Latino. "It just happened that way. And having them up front says a lot."

In some communities, you will learn that many are not in the country legally. You need to decide ahead of time how you will handle this reality. Clearly a church should not hire an illegal immigrant. However, different churches make different choices where to draw the line beyond this point. Some will not allow illegal immigrants to serve in any leadership position, while other churches choose not to ask people's legal status unless they are considering employment.

Once you set a standard, you have to back it up. Colleen Conti, network/campus development assistant at Healing Place, said, "You can't set a standard unless you are willing to say that this is the Scripture behind it and this is how we can help you sustain it."

Blake Lindsey summarized the approach of Church of the Highlands: "[Those without documentation] are all around us, and we are going to become a light to that community. We are not going to put limitations on who can attend and who can't attend based on that."

Conti added, "Serving is one of our core values, so if somebody is just interested in being involved and being invested and being a volunteer and they want to serve with their time, talent, and treasure, we don't want to hold them back from that."

The knowledge sharing that Leadership Network encouraged among first-generation multi-site churches has helped the multi-site movement grow quickly. It is fitting that the final piece of firsthand advice comes from the director of their research department, Warren Bird. Bird is coauthor of *The Multi-Site Church Revolution* (Zondervan, 2006) and continues to provide multi-site research at www.leadnet.org/multisiteresources.

Warren Bird

director of research, Leadership Network

More and more people today are drawn to the idea of hybrid cars. They understand the general idea—using two or more forms of power to improve fuel economy and reduce pollution. That perspective alone persuades many that hybrids are the right direction to go. But while they've seen ads for hybrid cars, they don't yet own one, nor have they even driven one. They don't realize that hybrids are not identical to the kind of car they're used to. They have an important learning curve ahead, and no doubt a few surprises as well.

Mark DeYmaz, author of *Building a Healthy Multi-Ethnic Church: Mandate, Commitments, and Practices of a Diverse Congregation*, uses this hybrid analogy when talking with church leaders who want to plant a multi-ethnic church. They find it to be a compelling idea—in fact Mark's book makes the case for "the biblical mandate for the multi-ethnic church," but as with a hybrid car, they've often not experienced one up close, nor do they realize that it's a bit different from a church where one ethnic group makes up the overwhelming majority.[4]

In my experience, the same thing happens when a church wants to cross cultures in order to add a new campus. There's good theology for doing so, but it's not as easy or simple as working with the kind of people they already know.

Drawing from research found in sociologist George Yancey's book *One Body, One Spirit*, DeYmaz adapts and restates seven general principles of successful multi-racial *churches*.[5] They likewise serve as solid advice when launching an ethnic or multi-cultural *campus:*

1. Embrace dependence
2. Take intentional steps
3. Empower diverse leadership

4. Develop cross-cultural relationships
5. Pursue cross-cultural competence
6. Promote a spirit of inclusion
7. Mobilize for impact

Start with Whom God Has Already Brought You

Those seven principles apply whether you're an African-American congregation planting a Creole-speaking Haitian campus, a Mandarin-speaking Chinese congregation planting a Cantonese-dialect campus, or a largely Caucasian congregation reaching out to the Polish-speaking community on the other side of town.

For multi-site congregations, the best starting point is the people already in your church, especially your staff and primary layleaders. What's their ethnic background? What languages and cultures do they move among most comfortably? What local cross-cultural connections do they have naturally? God is already at work in your community drawing all peoples to Himself (see John 12:32), and often all we need to do is to notice where He's already at work.

For example, I had lunch last week with a New Jersey pastor whose church plant meets in a neighborhood that's transitioning from English speakers to Spanish speakers. My friend, who is African-American, had celebrated from the church's opening day the diversity of ethnic backgrounds in the congregation, sponsoring a weekly after-church potluck where he encouraged people to bring their favorite Caribbean foods, soul foods, Tex-Mex foods, and other specialty dishes. He quickly noticed that the Latino foods were growing faster than any other segment, so he found a part-time bilingual associate pastor. This new pastor's presence and community interaction have caused the Latino element in the congregation to grow even more.

If you identify an ethnic group in your congregation and want to know how many people from that group live in your area, plug in your church's county or zip code at a Web site like www.peoplegroups.info (powered by the International and North American Mission Boards of the Southern Baptist Convention), and you can quickly identify the dominant ethnic groups in your community. Its easy-to-use lists are based on 2000 census data.

Allow for Relationship Building and Time

I think the most important success factor in launching an ethnic or multi-cultural site, beyond bathing everything in prayer, is to take the time necessary to build a strong, healthy relationship among the campuses' respective leadership teams. When Jesus brought together His twelve future apostles, who represented a wide range of backgrounds, the Scriptures observe that He had two initial goals: "that they might be with him and that he might send them out to preach" (Mark 3:14 NIV). You might say He wanted them to catch His heart (by being "with him") and He wanted them to stay connected with Him as they did ministry (when He would "send them out").

Dave Ferguson sets a good model for how to do this. As lead pastor, he, his younger brother Jon, and a few buddies from college started Community Christian Church in 1989. Sixteen years later they had grown to seven campuses. While each had mildly different socioeconomic levels, each site reached an English-speaking target audience.

In 2006 Community Christian launched its eighth location thirty miles away in the Pilsen neighborhood of Chicago—the largest Hispanic community east of Los Angeles. The campus pastor and staff are all fluent in both English and Spanish.

Dave's approach was to bring the future campus pastor, Eli Orozco, and his team onto Community Christian staff for more than a year before launching the new campus, which would minister in both English and Spanish. That time was spent building strong relationships with Orozco and his team, making sure they took on the reproducing DNA of the church. Then after the launch, the Community Christian Pilsen team would meet weekly in person or by conference call with Dave or other pastors from the various campuses. These meetings fit the leader-readiness emphasis of the church that is developed by maintaining an interpersonal rapport.

In addition to the leadership development meetings, the team from Community Christian Pilsen also works every week with other Community Christian campuses to develop the Big Idea creative content used at all sites, and then translates it into Spanish.[6]

Plan to Push Water Uphill

From the book of Acts onward church representatives from one culture, often called missionaries, have crossed language and cultural lines to plant self-supporting, self-governing, and self-replicating churches. These practices continue through today.

While church planting is consistently a hub for evangelism[7], a large majority of all churches, new and old, are mono-racial, where 80 percent or more of the individuals that attend are of the same ethnicity or race. This happens almost naturally as part of an "overwhelming push toward internal homogeneity."[8] According to data from the National Congregations Study, in 90 percent of American congregations, 90 percent of the members share the same race or ethnicity.[9]

Interestingly, the most multi-racial churches at present are the largest ones. *Beyond Megachurch Myths* by Scott Thumma and Dave Travis, reports on a major 2005 study of very large churches. It asks, "What is the total percentage of attenders in your church that are not of the majority racial/ethnic group?" The average was 19 percent. Some 36 percent have 20-percent minority presence or more.

The response to the next survey question was even more telling: "Is your congregation making efforts to become intentionally multi-ethnic?" A surprising 56 percent said yes.[10]

What about churches that are multi-site? Are they placing much emphasis on launching ethnic or multi-cultural sites? In "Leadership Network's 2007 Survey of 1,000 Multi-Site Churches," we asked for participants' primary motivation for doing multi-site. The overwhelming reply was "evangelism" (63 percent), although 1 percent did say "cross language or ethnic barriers."

We next asked their secondary motivation for doing multi-site. Of the same seven answer options, there was a two-way tie for first place: solve overcrowding (27 percent) and bring our church closer to a target area (also 27 percent). This time 4 percent said, "cross language or ethnic barriers"—and those churches were different from the 1 percent of churches who said this earlier. So a total of 5 percent of the churches indicate it's a top motivation. That's only one out of twenty cases.

Interestingly another set of questions asked, "Are you reaching the same kinds of people on each campus in terms of race?" Only 12 percent said yes. When asked, "Are you reaching the same kinds of people on each campus in terms of language?" Only 5 percent said yes.

The implications? At present, only a small percentage of churches are multi-ethnic. That includes multi-site churches as well. While the direction of change is toward multiple ethnicities, and most agree that's a healthy and biblical direction to move, for most it is a somewhat uphill process.

Experiment on a Small Scale

My first close-up exposure to local cross-cultural ministry occurred when I was in my early twenties. I was a deacon in a church that had opened its facilities to Cambodian and Haitian congregations, all of us from the same denomination. There was no relational connection between the three respective pastors or elder boards. The arrangement was at best one of sharing a building with occasional hurt feelings ("They sure stunk up the church kitchen" or "Their children messed up our new rock garden"). We deacons tried to change the relationship by hosting a get-to-know-one-another dinner. We invited each congregation to bring food, which we'd share with each other.

It was a well-motivated idea but awkward. Our announced 6:00 p.m. start time meant different things in different cultures, so we didn't all arrive together. There were major language differences as we sat with each other. While some of the food exchanges met with smiles, other samplings caused disappointment when not everyone affirmed one another's taste.

I think everyone was still glad we made the effort. It was a one-shot approach to building goodwill, and it worked. What if we, and especially the pastors themselves, had been more intentional? I bet the relationships could have gone a lot farther. Who knows where vision and ongoing leadership might have led us?

Likewise, anything you do to reach out cross-culturally will involve risk and steps into the unknown. It will probably do more good than harm. But before you commit to an ongoing major effort to launch an ethnic or cross-cultural site, it might be wise to test the waters by taking several low-risk, smaller scale steps.

Merging with or Absorbing an Existing Church

Since being called as Shelter Rock Church's pastor in 2002, Steve Tomlinson has led the church to be willing to change to share the gospel with their community. Their vision has expanded from reaching local Manhasset—their original name was Manhasset Baptist Church—to reaching all of Long Island.

Shelter Rock's initial move into multi-site was stimulated by barriers to growth. Three times each weekend Shelter Rock was filling their sanctuary that holds two hundred fifty. This building sits on a quarter of an acre, so expansion at that site was not an option. The cost of living on Long Island is one of the highest in the nation and land prices are equally debilitating.

In 2004 Shelter Rock began seriously to look for a location in which they could either plant a church or possibly start a new site. In asking questions, they caught wind of a church in their affiliation called Bible Baptist Church that was located twelve miles east of them in a neighborhood with very similar demographics. The church had a sanctuary that could seat 300, the church sat on 5 acres, and best of all they had parking spaces—120 of them! Despite all these physical resources, the church was down to eighteen people attending on a given Sunday.

Shelter Rock's leadership began meeting with the remaining leaders at Bible Baptist and they laid out a plan for a merger. This step-by-step plan provides a great road map when exploring such mergers:

Discussions between Leaders: Shelter Rock explained that Bible Baptist would need to close and join the work of Shelter Rock under Shelter Rock's leadership. Through a series of meetings, questions were answered and trust was established.

Official Offer to Receive the Closing Church: As both churches verbally agreed upon the plan, Shelter Rock voted that they were willing to receive Bible Baptist as part of their church. Bible Baptist's members knew that Shelter Rock had open arms to receive them.

Legal Closure: Bible Baptist Church would legally cease to exist. Shelter Rock asked that a super majority of members would need to approve this through their congregational form of government. They would assign their assets to Shelter Rock, and the members would join Shelter Rock. Bible Baptist did this in June 2005.

Emotional Closure: A farewell service was held at Bible Baptist Church to celebrate what God had done throughout its history and to bring closure to this church. They flew in the church's most successful pastor, Fred Mackey, who had served there in the 1970s. With one hundred fifty people in attendance they sang old hymns and Mackey gave an inspiring message.

Investment in Refurbishing Facility: The very next day, the work crews came in and began giving the facility a face-lift. This included new carpet, new drywall, and new lighting. Projection equipment was added, individual chairs replaced the pews, and the library was converted to a café.

Launch New Site: Shelter Rock had a kickoff service there on September 18, 2005, with two hundred seventy people in attendance. (They did conduct one practice service the week before.) Attendees came from three sources. Roughly a third came from the Manhasset location, a third were old Bible Baptist attendees, and a third were curious neighbors. They had invested in local newspaper ads and signs in train stations to get the word out.

For Shelter Rock, using mergers with dying or struggling churches makes a lot of stewardship sense for both financial and time reasons. Tomlinson shared, "Many of our people work in New York City, and they don't get home until nine o'clock at night. The idea of them packing a church every Sunday—I just don't see a lot of people willing to do that. But if we could have a facility that we have exclusive use over, they are willing to do that. So we have been more interested in looking at dying churches than just renting a hotel room or something."

Using the same six steps, here are some additional bits of advice related to launching a site based on a merger with another church.

Discussions between Leaders

Guy Melton, pastor of Oasis Church, describes the early discussions Oasis had with First Baptist Church of North Miami.

It's been a three- or four-month process, most of it behind the scenes, meeting with people, meeting with our own people, meeting with their people. . . . We believe it is a God thing. We didn't go out looking for it.

Most older churches I have found, quite frankly, would rather die than to merge with another church and lose their identity or their name. But I believe it is the way to go. I believe they have done a wise thing because now their ministry will go on for decades.

I've told each of these people as I have visited in their homes—some of them are so sick they don't even get to church much anymore,— "You know what? It will look totally different. It will sound different. You won't necessarily like everything we do, but one thing I want you to hear me say is that it is the same exact mission you started with eighty-two years ago and it goes back to Matthew 28, the mission Jesus Christ gave us, and we will

> *You won't necessarily like everything we do, but one thing I want you to hear me say is that it is the same exact mission you started with eighty-two years ago and it goes back to Matthew 28, the mission Jesus Christ gave us, and we will be as passionate about that as your church was when it started eighty-two years ago.*

be as passionate about that as your church was when it started eighty-two years ago."

Tomlinson described the type of meeting this is with the remaining elders or leaders of the dying church. "What we will do is we will have a gut-honest-level conversation, which will very politely say they will cease to exist if they want to come with us."

Mark Estep, pastor of Spring Baptist Church, was equally forthright in sharing the implications with Bridgestone Baptist Church. "I made it very clear to them that this is hook, line, and sinker. You lose your name. You lose your titles. Your deacons will no longer be deacons. They will come under our bylaws and our bylaws require that you have to be a member of our church for a minimum of a year before you can be considered to be a deacon."

In a very real way a struggling church is being revitalized. Chuck Carter, pastor at First Baptist Windermere, refers to this as a "rescue church" or a "resurrection model." A dead church is getting new life.

Tomlinson indicated that in these discussions "we will use language that is polite. We will call it a merger. It is a merger into nonexistence, however." The old guard from the closing church will not be coddled. The church will be consumed with reaching people for Jesus Christ. "We will not try to make Mr. So-and-so happy so he doesn't have a heart attack. . . . They have to own what we are going to do and then they have to agree that it is now Shelter Rock. It is not them."

Official Offer to Receive the Closing Church

Estep stressed the importance of the meetings before the meeting in which the decision is made. In many congregational churches, this final meeting involves a vote. Estep listed the meetings beforehand. "I met with the trustees. They were unanimous about moving forward. Then I met with the deacons here at my church. They were unanimous that we should move forward. I then held small group meetings here with our congregation for people who had questions about it." All of these leaders were present to help answer questions during three separate question-and-answer times for the congregation. The story was also printed up for the congregation as they considered it.

As Shelter Rock considers future mergers, the leadership seeks to keep this before the congregation so they are prepared when it happens. "This past Sunday was a vision message," Tomlinson said. "We started talking about the fact that two churches have approached us. We didn't tell them what churches. We didn't tell them that we were going to say yes. Honestly, we don't know if we are going to say yes. But we want them to keep hearing that is going to happen."

Legal Closure

Cedar Park Church became a multi-site church because they did not want to see another church in their denomination (Assembly of God) close their doors. Senior associate pastor Craig Gorc summarized the process: "What we did was we actually dissolved the corporation and their assets became our assets. Then based upon that, we took out a new loan and refinanced that property."

Legally, what we are describing is not a merger. The key advantage legally to dissolving the struggling church is that any legal liabilities from that church, known or unknown, dissolve with that church. Estep emphasized, "You must seek legal advice. Make sure you do things legally not only for the health of your main campus, but also for the health and protection of the second campus that you are about to take over."

Then whatever assets the church owns can be given to the multi-site church. If a balance is still owed on the property, then it is typically sold to the multi-site church for the balance of the loan.

As the church dissolves, whatever paid staff the church has are then unemployed. It is up to the multi-site church to decide whether they want to hire any existing staff members. As Shelter Rock demonstrated when they chose not to hire a staff member, it is a noble thing to offer the unhired staff member severance pay.

Emotional Closure

Tomlinson talked about the value of momentum that the multi-site church brings to the church that is closing. "For these dying churches, you dilute whatever was sick about them. Small churches are sick because they are small. Too many people have too much say at a meeting. That is all diluted when you join a larger group. So a lot of those things just fade away."

Because such emotional closure is difficult, you may expect it to take a long time. However, a different emotional element will take over as the site begins to reach people. Tomlinson describes the buy-in to giving up the old to reach the lost that he has seen seniors achieve. "I have seen them weep. We got a wonderful letter last week from a woman from Syosset campus that said, 'Pastor Jerry has to install tissue boxes in the parking lot, because every time I drive to church now I start weeping when I see all the cars here.'

"Another woman came to me on picnic Sunday and said, 'I have to tell you, Pastor Steve, what happened.' She mentioned this woman who came up to her and this woman said, 'Fran, Fran, I sat in the balcony today.' And she said, 'So?' 'No. You don't understand. I *had* to sit in the balcony today!' And she was weeping when she said this because these people who were left—the remaining eighteen—are so blown away when they can't get a seat in church."

Investment in Refurbishing Facility

Guy Melton, pastor of Oasis Church, describes what they learned as they merged with First Baptist Church of North Miami. "We decided it's better to go slower. It's a little bit more painful on the front end—not quite the instant gratification at the front end. But we believe in going slower and in making that a [time of] preparation of the building and the people that are part of who we are along with the leadership that understand who we are. We'll be far better in the long run."

Melton said, "We're going to call it an 'extreme church makeover.' We are going to totally redo the inside of the building. We are going to totally redo the grounds. Totally—I mean just take them down to the bare walls and the bare dirt outside so that when the community is invited, we are ready for them and prepared."

Launch New Site

Tomlinson noted, "We immediately started with two services. We wanted to start a culture by which the idea is that you serve in one service and attend another service."

Shelter Rock also learned that they needed to staff the church during the week. "Because this church had a history, people like to know that they can just stop by the church and visit and know that there is a live body there."

Melton shared the following story of how God had prepared Oasis for their merger with First Baptist North Miami.

When we started our church, it was an eighty-plus-year-old church that was our sponsor in Miami. And it's only about four miles from [First Baptist North Miami]. And it's on the same road, Dixie Highway, ironically. And after a year it was a dying church, about thirty people, just like this one. The neighborhood had changed. The people had basically moved out of the area or died. And they sponsored us, and in about a year they decided, "You know what? We're just spinning our wheels. We're going to sell this building and give the proceeds to the Pines Church [now Oasis Church], because they are reaching people like we are not and they are baptizing people like we are not and this money would go better [there]."

They have taken those thirty people and now we are ministering to more than two thousand people every week with what they

---

did. And so that church didn't die, and it's a wonderful thing. And the people that are still with us that are elderly say, "You know, it's just wonderful even though it's so different compared to what we ever had. We see people being baptized and people being saved and lives changed." They love it.

Ironically that's how we got our start. We were able to take much of that money to start and build the building we're in and now to take a lot of that money and put it toward the Hollywood campus. And then the Hollywood campus will be paying us back that money so that we can put it into future campuses. So it's really these two older churches that, in some ways, have allowed us to extend the kingdom even though they were down to thirty people, about to die in eighty-year-old situations.

Two multi-site churches described much larger mergers. Life Church.tv had a large church, Metro Church, approach them about coming together. Many years ago Metro had been a very large church. It had declined over the years but was relatively stable or plateaued with attendance around six hundred when they approached LifeChurch. "They really felt like being a part of LifeChurch would bring new growth and momentum and take the building and resources that God had entrusted them with and invest it. They felt like it would be a better kingdom return after that investment."

The Chapel is another example of a church that has conducted a merger with a large church rather than one that is about to disappear. Mergers of any two organizations include merging processes but more importantly cultures. In the world of corporate mergers, much money must be budgeted to move to a single set of processes. Yet the long-term health of the merged corporation often rests more on the culture that emerges than its process flows. Research has shown that the greatest predictor of success in merging corporate cultures is having an intentional plan.

While The Chapel's merger with a church of eight hundred people did not allow much time for formal plans, there was intentionality. In fact, copastor Scott Chapman wore a second hat for a year and served as their campus pastor. "I wanted to personally let them know that they were not a stepchild and that I was going to treat them as a child."

This process required many, many meetings to work through the logistics of how things are done and the style in which the site would function. Chapman summarized, "That is still my campus home. My family attends that campus. And so we relationally committed and it worked."

Merging church cultures is also an issue for the more typical merger that is restoring a very small or dying church. While it is clear up front that the culture of the multi-site church will be the surviving culture, it still requires intentionality to bring members of the now closed church into this culture.

"I was talking to one of the guys that used to be a deacon there," Estep shared. "I said, 'Isn't it great what God is doing? We have baptized twelve people, and—praise the Lord—He's done it! And the Lord sent eighteen people to join in the last couple months.' And he said, 'Yeah, yeah, that's really good. But when are we going to replace that carpet around the stage there? It looks pretty shoddy.'"

Estep noticed that "small churches sometimes do things that may be unintentional that create an attitude and an air of smallness. . . . The most natural thing in the world is to get your eye off of and your mind off of why you really exist in the first place. Your existence becomes more about physical, tangible things as opposed to spiritual things."

Epilogue

Naysayers shake their heads at the multi-site movement, wondering out loud why a church would want to have multiple locations, if it is in their best interest to keep their sites as one church in the long term, or if somehow multi-site is bad.

The answers to these questions begin with Jesus Christ's teaching on identifying the bad and the good: "For each tree is known by its own fruit" (Luke 6:44).

The pattern that so clearly emerges from the multi-site churches interviewed reveals a heart that is focused on the kingdom of God. Their stories show that God first blessed the churches with evangelistic effectiveness. Then as they sought to be good stewards of these blessings, God opened doors of opportunity for them to become multi-site.

Then God continued to use these churches to reach new people in new places as members and staff selflessly invested in new work. The fruit has been abundantly good.

In the end multi-site is a tool. It is a tool to use at God's leading that can be seen in His movement within a church and in His provision of a campus pastor, a core group, a location, systems and structures, and finances. As God spreads this burden and as leadership agrees on this strategic direction, then a church should not hesitate to become multi-site.

Instead they should use multi-site to its fullest potential. The first and second generation multi-site churches shared their challenges with you to help you do just that.

Each church added new insights but also could have benefited from principles shared by other multi-site churches. May God use their guidance to allow fewer to stumble over multi-site strategy and implementation so more people in more places will hear the gospel.

Multi-site churches reveal a tiny glimpse of how vast the church of Jesus Christ is as some use simultaneous worship, overseas campuses, large geographic vision, and sheer numbers of sites. Yet the multi-site movement is only one small piece of God's movement through His church to share the gospel of Jesus Christ with the entire world. His movement is not limited to a form, a style, a location, a time, a size, or a method.

May God be praised as you consider His movement in multi-site churches today and may He expand your vision for what He can do in and through you and your church.

Notes

1. Tom Van Riper, "Wal-Mart Nation," www.Forbes.com, January 30, 2007.

2. Thom S. Rainer and Eric Geiger, *Simple Church* (Nashville, TN: Broadman & Homan Publishers, 2006), 20.

3. Ibid., 60.

4. Mark DeYmaz, *Building a Healthy Multi-Ethnic Church: Mandate, Commitments, and Practices of a Diverse Congregation* (San Francisco, CA: Jossey-Bass, 2007), 41.

5. George Yancey, *One Body, One Spirit* (Downer's Grove, IL: InterVarsity Press, 2003).

6. Dave Ferguson, Jon Ferguson, and Eric Bramlett, *The Big Idea: Focus the Message, Multiply the Impact* (Grand Rapids, MI: Zondervan, 2007).

7. See Leadership Network's massive research project, State of Church Planting USA, by Ed Stetzer.

8. Michael O. Emerson and Christian Smith, *Divided by Faith* (Oxford: Oxford University Press, 2000), 136.

9. Mark Chaves, et al., "The National Congregations Study: Background, Methods, and Selected Results," *Journal for the Scientific Study of Religion* 38(4): 458–76.

10. Scott Thumma and Dave Travis, *Beyond Megachurch Myths* (San Francisco, CA: Jossey-Bass, 2007). See also http://hirr.hartsem.edu/megachurch/megastoday2005detaileddate.pdf, 6.

Person Interviewed	Title of Person at Time of Interview	Church Name
Barry Galloway	Campus Pastor	Desert Vineyard Christian Fellowship
Barry Smith	Senior Pastor	Impact Community Church
Blake Lindsey	Campus Pastor	Church of the Highlands
Bobby Gruenewald	Innovation Pastor	LifeChurch.tv
Brodie Taphorn	Community Leader	Upper Arlington Lutheran Church
Chuck Babler	Campus Pastor	Crossroads Community Church
Chuck Carter	Pastor	First Baptist Church Windermere
Colleen Conti	Development Assistant	Healing Place Church
Craig Gorc	Senior Associate	Cedar Park Church
Dan Ohlerking	Lead Pastor Team	Healing Place Church
Dan Scates	Multi-Site Minister	LifeBridge Christian Church
Dave Browning	Lead Pastor	Christ the King Community Church International
Dave Lonsberry	Executive Director of Business and Finance	Christ Fellowship
David McDaniel	Director of North Point Ministries	North Point Community Church
David Parker	Lead Pastor	Desert Vineyard Christian Fellowship
Don Ruppenthal	Associate Pastor	RiverTree Christian Church
David McKinley	Teaching Pastor	Prestonwood Baptist Church
Drew Hayes	Lead Pastor	The People's Church
Guy Melton	Senior Pastor	Oasis Church
Jamie Wamsley	Associate Pastor	The Chapel
Jason Cullum	Lead Pastor	Christ's Church
Jim Carrie	Executive & Missions/Outreach Pastor	Chartwell Baptist Church
Joe Stowell	Executive Pastor	Harvest Bible Church

Person Interviewed	Title of Person at Time of Interview	Church Name
Joey White	Campus Pastor	First Baptist Church McKinney
Kathy Chapman Sharp	Executive Pastor of Communications	The Chapel
Katie Moore	Director of Communications & Public Relations	LifeChurch.tv
Keith Boyer	Lead Pastor	Crossroads Community Church
Kevin Penry	Pastor, Operational Leader	LifeChurch.tv
Larry Ali	Executive Pastor	Desert Vineyard Christian Fellowship
Larry Osborne	Senior Pastor	North Coast Church
Marc Cleary	Lead Pastor Team	Healing Place Church
Mark Bankford	Directional Leader	Heartland Community Church
Mark Batterson	Lead Pastor	National Community Church
Mark Estep	Senior Pastor	Spring Baptist Church
Mark Stermer	Campus Development Pastor	Healing Place Church
Michelle Cox	Administrative Assistant	Crossroads Community Church
Mike Bickley	Lead Pastor	Olathe Bible Church
Mike Brisson	Associate Pastor	Cornerstone Community Church
Mike Hurt	Director of Community Campus Development	McLean Bible Church
Mike Ladra	Senior Pastor	First Presbyterian Church
Mike Miller	Director of Ministry Support	Community Presbyterian Church
Nathan Lewis	Pastor	Evergreen Presbyterian Church
Owen Nease	Campus Pastor	Henderson Hills
Neil Nakamoto	International Liaison	Mosaic
Robbie Stewart	Campus Pastor	Northview Christian Life Church

Person Interviewed	Title of Person at Time of Interview	Church Name
Ron Vietti	Senior Pastor	Valley Bible Fellowship
Scott Chapman	Co-Senior Pastor	The Chapel
Steve Tomlinson	Senior Pastor	Shelter Rock Church
Stovall Weems	Lead Pastor	Celebration Church
Tim Davis	Guest Relations & Multi-Site Director	Woodcrest Chapel
Tim Tracey	Executive Director of Worship	Northland, A Church Distributed
Anonymous	Anonymous	Anonymous

Church Name	Pastor	Web site
Anonymous	Anonymous	Anonymous
Cedar Park Church Bothell, Washington	Joseph Fuiten Senior Pastor	www.cedarpark.org
Celebration Church Jacksonville, Florida	Stovall Weens Lead Pastor	www.celebration.org
Chartwell Baptist Church Oakville, Ontario	Andrew Gordon Teaching Pastor	www.chartwellchurch.org
Christ's Church Jacksonville, Florida	Jason Cullum Lead Pastor	www.ccontheweb.com
Christ Fellowship Palm Beach Garden, Florida	Tom Mullins Senior Pastor	www.gochristfellowship.com
Christ the King Community Church Burlington, Washington	Dave Browning Lead Pastor	www.ctkonline.com
Church of the Highlands Birmingham, Alabama	Chris Hodges Pastor	www.churchoftheHighlands.com
Community Presbyterian Church Danville, California	Scott Farmer Senior Pastor	www.cpcdanville.org
Cornerstone Community Church Wildomar, California	Ron Armstrong Senior Pastor	www.go2cornerstone.com
Crossroads Community Church Freeport, Illinois	Keith Boyer Lead Pastor	www.crossroadscn.com
Desert Vineyard Christian Fellowship Lancaster, California	David Parker Lead Pastor	www.desertvineyard.org
Evergreen Presbyterian Church Beaverton, Oregon	Nathan Lewis Pastor	www.evergreenpca.com
First Baptist Church McKinney McKinney, Texas	Jeff Warren Lead Pastor	www.fbcmckinney.com
First Baptist Church Windermere Windermere, Florida	Chuck Carter Pastor	www.fbcwindermere.com
First Presbyterian Church Salinas, California	Mike Ladra Senior Pastor	www.fpcsalinas.org
Harvest Bible Chapel Rolling Meadows, Illinois	James MacDonald Senior Pastor	www.harvestbiblechapel.org
Healing Place Church Baton Rouge, Louisiana	Dino and DeLynn Rizzo Pastors	www.healingplacechurch.org
Heartland Community Church Rockford, Illinois	Doug Thiesen Lead Pastor	www.heartland.cc

Church Name	Pastor	Web site
Henderson Hills Edmond, Oklahoma	Dennis Newkirk Teaching Pastor	www.hhbc.com
Impact Community Church Sacramento, California	Barry Smith Senior Pastor	www.impact.cc
LifeBridge Christian Church Longmont, Colorado	Rick Rusaw Senior Minister	www.lbcc.org
LifeChurch.tv Edmond, Oklahoma	Craig Groeschel Senior Pastor	www.lifechurch.tv
McLean Bible Church McLean, Virginia	Lon Solomon Senior Pastor	www.mcleanbible.org
Mosaic Pasadena, California	Erwin McManus Lead Navigator	www.mosaic.org
National Community Church Washington, D.C.	Mark Batterson Lead Pastor	www.theaterchurch.com
North Coast Church Vista, California	Larry Osborne Senior Pastor	www.northcoastchurch.com
North Point Community Church Alpharetta, Georgia	Andy Stanley Senior Pastor	www.northpoint.org
Northland, A Church Distributed Longwood, Florida	Joel Hunter Senior Pastor	www.northlandchurch.net
Northview Christian Life Church Carmel, Indiana	Steve Poe Lead Pastor	www.nvcl.org
Oasis Church Pembroke Pines, Florida	Guy Melton Senior Pastor	www.visitoasis.org
Olathe Bible Church Olathe, Kansas	Mike Bickley Lead Pastor	www.olathebible.org
Prestonwood Baptist Church Plano, Texas	Jack Graham Pastor	www.prestonwood.org
RiverTree Christian Church Massillon, Ohio	Greg Nettle Senior Pastor	www.rivertreechristian.com
Shelter Rock Church Manhasset, New York	Steve Tomlinson Senior Pastor	www.shelterrockchurch.com
Spring Baptist Church Spring, Texas	Mark Estep Senior Pastor	www.springbaptist.org
The Chapel Libertyville, Illinois	Scott Chapman and Jeff Griffin, Co-Senior Pastors	www.chapel.org

Church Name	Pastor	Web site
The People's Church Shelbyville, Tennessee	Drew Hayes Lead Pastor	www.peopleschurchshelbyville.org
Upper Arlington Lutheran Church Columbus, Ohio	Paul Ulring Senior Pastor	http://ualc.org
Valley Bible Fellowship Bakersfield, California	Ron Vietti Senior Pastor	www.vbf.org
Woodcrest Chapel Columbia, Missouri	Pieter Van Waarde Senior Pastor	www.woodcrest.org

More research-based books by
B&H Publishing Group
and LifeWay Research